Balada de la Sangre

Los Poemas de
María Elena Cruz Varela

TRADUCIDOS POR
MAIRYM CRUZ-BERNAL CON DEBORAH DIGGES

Ballad of the Blood

The Poems of
María Elena Cruz Varela

TRANSLATED BY
MAIRYM CRUZ-BERNAL WITH DEBORAH DIGGES

THE ECCO PRESS

THE ECCO PRESS
100 West Broad Street
Hopewell, New Jersey 08525

Published simultaneously in Canada
by Penguin Books Canada Ltd., Ontario

Printed in the United States of America

Library of Congress Cataloging-in-Publication Data
Cruz Varela, María Elena, 1953–
      [Poems.   English & Spanish]
      Ballad of the blood : the poems of María Elena Cruz Varela /
   translated by Mairym Cruz-Bernal with Deborah Digges. — 1st ed.
         p.   cm.
      ISBN 0-88001-427-X
      1. Cruz Varela, María Elena, 1953–   — Translations into English.
   I. Cruz-Bernal, Mairym.   II. Digges, Deborah.   III. Title.
   PQ7390.C73A23   1995
   861 – dc20   95-22796

Designed by Fearn Cutler de Vicq de Cumptich

The text of this book is set in Didot
9 8 7 6 5 4 3 2 1
FIRST EDITION

Contents

Preface

There is the poetry of rivers—gravity's genius—whose meander takes its direction from the earth's motion, from the narrative carved out millennia ago, the narrative in place, the assumed story, by its coursing oceanic, overlapping, dispersed and dispersing. "Flow on, river! flow with the flood-tide," writes Whitman. And in Auden's elegy to Yeats, the poetry of rivers, "Makes nothing happen . . . flows on south / From ranches of isolation and the busy griefs, / Raw towns that we believe and die in; It survives, / A way of happening, mouth . . . "

And there is poetry that is anything but rivers, though the nature of rivers may be, in part, necessary for its resistance. It is a poetry that flies against time, ". . . Against the fear of the man that creeps. Whistles. Spits again. Curses . . . Against you . . . Against my darkest side. Against gentle water," writes Maria Elena Cruz Varela. Such poetry defies gravity. Its existence depends on countermotion, subversion, suspension, and it must do more than merely *survive* lyric collisions with history, with social and political systems that would erase it, erase the voices that sing in spite of it. It must make art of that collision.

Varela's work subjugates context—prison, suffering, exile—and pushes beyond mere images of despair into the visionary, the voice stripped, the language attenuated. If there is a precedent for Varela, it is eclectic, international, historic. Like Dickinson, Tsvetaeva, Akhmatova, Levi, and Celan, Varela's poems retain qualities of the echo, of one voice shattered into many, like songs in rags, lyrics that haunt sleep, particular, peculiar, anonymous. Inside them is a mortal moaning, like the rafters where the rope hung from one of the huge nails used to hold horse collars takes suddenly Tsvetaeva's full weight.

Inside her poems we hear many voices, the voices of the cast out and the silenced, the tortured and freed, tortured and returned to cells, and the ones executed, thrown into common graves and forgotten. In *Ballad of the Blood* Varela lifts these voices up to us, caged as they are in time, lifts them into myth where they are better buried, named and buried and remembered. Now they are Philomela, Hagar singing in the wilderness her death lullaby, Dickinson's "strange Race wrecked, solitary," and the whisperings of Akhmatova's "Woman with blue lips," who stands beside the poet in a queue outside the Gulag in Leningrad. "Can you describe this?" she asks. Akhmatova answers, "Yes, I can." Varela's poems are the breath gone out of us, a broken silence that owes nothing to history, nor to the translators. It is our duty simply to get out of the way.

Deborah Digges

Introduction

"... says only: this is a picture of all life, and from it learn the meaning of your life. And conversely; read only your life and understand from it the hieroglyphics of universal life."

—NIETZSCHE

The first night I stayed at María Elena's house in Havana, she told me in vivid detail an account of November 21, 1991. Friends were used to make her open her door, and when she did, she was pushed, face-first, into the wall, her arms pinned behind her. Her intruders dragged her down the stairs and into the street. In public view, the *Brigadas de Acción* tried to force her to eat the manifesto she had written, signed, and distributed the previous day, a manifesto that echoed a document she had submitted a year before to the president of the State Council. María Elena had composed the document to reflect the feelings of the *Criterio Alternativo*, an intellectual opposition group to which she belonged. The document was sent on November 15, 1990, the day marking the thirty-first anniversary of the Cuban revolution:

> Because I am a rational being, conscious of my
> individuality and prudent of mind, I absolutely refuse, with
> the only weapon at my disposal (the only weapon that
> interests me and that I consider effectual: The Word), to
> participate in what I consider to be a "closed system of
> impossibilities," a system that recognizes submission to a
> crude ideology, in which antagonism has the upper hand, as
> its only alternative. The noun "dead" is used far more
> frequently than its antonym "life"; the same holds true for
> war and peace, hate and love.... Like the responsibility one
> has when writing books that are evaluated and read by
> others, I feel responsible for the "role" I willingly assume at
> this historical moment. My standpoint is: NO, I DO NOT

AGREE. Experimenting with the lives of millions of people must be stopped. This is my manifesto.

María Elena described to me how, refusing to open her mouth, she clenched her teeth until she could taste her own blood, could see it flow onto her shirt. But as her accusers cursed and beat her she remained silent. Six days after her arrest, a closed trial was held; the official charges against her, "illegal association and libel."

María Elena's accounts of the arrest blurred with stories of her subsequent imprisonment, blurred with her cell mates' stories, some of which would later find their way into her poems, and some that would not—among them a fellow inmate's dispassionate report to María Elena that she had strangled her newborn because she couldn't stand the sound of the crying. María Elena recalled her own fourteen-year-old son's first visit to see her. Soon I would learn from the poet's family that our initial meeting marked the first time María Elena had spoken to anyone of her two years in prison. As yet a stranger to her, I had become the person through whom she could, as she later described it, exorcise the demons of her memory. "The Poet saved me," said María Elena.

I had arrived in Havana on Sunday, September 19, 1993, and met María Elena shortly after. I had never known anyone like her. Her intensity made me drunk. I couldn't follow her eyes, the movements of her head, the energy and desperation with which she spoke. As I listened to her I felt she might fly to the window and jump. I found myself studying the windows' sizes and proportions. Many times I nearly stood to close them, although the humidity was overwhelming. Then I wanted to close the windows with my eyes. I was suddenly a believer in magic.

The woman who sat with me now in the close heat of a Havana night wore no makeup, no high heels. An extraordinarily sensual woman, she wore a yellow blouse opened down the back. Three ribbons, one below the other, gathered her shirt at her waist. As she spoke, the shoulder of her blouse would fall down her arm. "I didn't decide to be a woman or a Cuban or a poet. I only chose to be a mother twice," she repeated. "It's been twelve years since I wrote my first verse, a tacky verse! But I have always, always lived like a poet, like this, the way you see me, the way you feel me."

María Elena repeated words and phrases, as if she were reteaching herself the truth, as if the language itself must be intensified, hammered and hammered out, made lyric. I remember her words, her precise diction, so much that was said during our first hours together. Chronicled here, the white space of the page around her words fragments her speech and frustrates me, frustrates all that was forced by her passion and her intelligence and her need.

She said,

> You don't know how happy I am that you came here
> because of my poetry . . . .
> I am not leaving Cuba because I feel historically obliged,
> because as a poet I have to stay here, with my people, I don't
> believe in exile for me. It exists, but not for me . . . .
> There are opponents that do not oppose. I am not one of
> those, but I don't judge them either . . . .
> I am imprisoned by a system that gives me no
> alternatives . . . .
> I belong to my people, not toward the history of a
> hundred years from now, but in the history of the moment we
> live today. . . .

María Elena Cruz Varela was born on a farm called Laberinto (Labyrinth) in Colón, a province of Matanzas. Her parents were *campesinos*, and her education, therefore, is entirely self-taught. The two years of her imprisonment merely suspended a long struggle for this young Cuban poet who had, by the time I met her, already authored three books of poems. The first two, *Mientras la espera el agua* (*While the Water Waits for Her*, 1986) and *Afuera está lloviendo* (*It's Raining Outside*, 1987), had been published in Cuba by Letras Cubanas. Nothing remains of the former, the copies confiscated and destroyed. A third book, *El Angel Agotado* (*The Exhausted Angel*), was published in Spain in 1991 and sold in Miami, though María Elena never saw any of the proceeds, royalties, or reviews.

During the years before her imprisonment, however, her work had not gone unnoticed. In 1989 she received an award from the

National Union of Cuban Writers and Artists (NUCWA) for her, as yet unpublished, collection of poems *Hija de Eva* (*Daughter of Eve*). But that organization threw her out in 1991. Prior to the Pan-American Games in Havana in September of that year, to prevent her from talking to the international press, she was placed under house arrest. In spite of her incarceration, and just before the Fourth Party Congress, María Elena did meet with foreign journalists and she spoke out for social and economic changes in Cuba. The following day the *Brigadas de Acción Rápida*, a group of civilians recruited by the government to hold spontaneous demonstrations in front of the homes of dissidents, broke into María Elena's home.

Throughout the centuries, writers and artists have confined themselves in different ways—Ovidio's exile, Proust's cork-panelled rooms. Poets, by trade, are introspective and such introspection can become merely self-imposed isolation. In María Elena's case, however, that isolation was rigorously imposed by others, and she would explain to me that such censorship produced in her a suffocation, a scream she could not hold any longer. She told me of her experiences as a condemned poet without self-pity. Hers was a narrative out of the mouth of an angel, a terrible angel. María Elena spent one year and eight months in prison. Then, "I left the small prison to enter the big one." She had just turned forty.

On the second day of our meeting in Havana, María Elena gave me her entire work, a manuscript including many unpublished poems, exquisite poems. Later, reading and rereading those poems in my own hotel room, I'd look up to the windows that overlooked the Atlantic, open my eyes wide to face the magnitude of the ocean, its blues and violets and greens. Between the poems and the sea, I thought I had encountered *el paraíso*. María Elena's poems written and preserved against censorship, humiliations, beatings, and imprisonment, constitute *Ballad of the Blood*, now given to the world. The survival of this work is evidence of what can happen to the imagination during times of extreme adversity, and evidence that in spite of adversity, the universal spirit seeks freedom. María Elena's poetry, indeed, was the only place she could be free. As she said during our first hours together, "*The Poet saved me.*"

Now the world has begun to recognize and celebrate these poems. María Elena has been adopted as an honorary member of the eight P.E.N. organizations and has been admitted into the International P.E.N. Club. In 1993 she was awarded the Poetry International Prize in Holland. She was granted permission to leave Cuba in May of 1994 to visit Washington, D.C., where she received the Liberty Prize from Liberal International. María Elena Cruz Varela now lives temporarily in Puerto Rico with her daughter. She lives not as an exile, but as one granted permission to work as Visiting Poet at the Inter-American University of Puerto Rico. Her son remains in Cuba.

Mairym Cruz-Bernal
January 25, 1995
San Juan, Puerto Rico

Ballad of the Blood

Bajo el paso del fuego

Digan que estoy cansada, que soy buena
que he vendido en subasta mi agonía
que se gastó la sal en mis arenas
y que pongo a secar la vida mía.

Digan que la humedad me tuvo muerta
que es muy triste bañarse con cenizas
que regalé las flores de mi huerta
y el último botón de mi camisa.

Y díganle también que se suicidan
objetos personales en mi cama
que destilo la luz por las heridas
y escribo este papel sobre la llama.

Under the Passage of Fire

Say that I am tired, that I am good,
that I've sold through auctions my agony,
that there are no more salts on my sands,
that I put away my very life.

Say that the humidity found me dead,
that it is sad to bathe with ashes,
that I gave away my garden flowers
and the last button on my shirt.

And say to him also that on my bed
personal objects are committing suicide,
that I distill light through my wounds
and that I write this poem over the fire.

El salto

Vuelve a saltar, Antinoo. Esa es tu vocación.
Develar entre rocas el misterio acucioso de tu carne.
Liturgia que se escapa. Detalle incomprensible.
Destrozar la belleza.
Mostrar la masa sin amor. Sanguinolenta.
Salpicando los riscos.
Antinoo está saltando. Se estrella en lo más hondo de sí mismo.
Con él saltamos todos. Y toda la miseria del no ser.
Toda la mansedumbre. Todo el asco. Toda esta poquedad
cabe en tu hermoso cuerpo de cautivo.
Punzada el adjetivo. Punzada es la pobreza de nombrarte.
Sí, cuando abrazo a un hombre, abrazo lo más viejo de este mito.
Abrazo su pasado. Rociándole a las fieras los miembros
del futuro y del presente.
Así, mientras tú saltas, te contemplo.
Todo salta contigo. Te comtemplo. Empujándote
con la fuerza siniestra de toda nuestra raza sin destino.
Es tan sólo saltar. Como si nada.
Aprendiendo caminos.
Desoladoramente irresponsables. La pistola caliente
en la entreabierta boca del cautivo.
A media noche el salto.
Siempre es el mismo salto hacia lo mismo.
Antinoo está saltando. Con él saltamos todos.
Dulce es la vocación de los suicidas. Dejarse devorar.
Saltar contigo en una sucesión de contingencias.
Mi salto no es más nuevo con los siglos.
Si cuando un hombre salta, con él se estrellan todos.
Todos quedamos rotos. Esparcidos.
La pureza se alcanza con el salto.
Abajo están las piedras. Las tentadoras piedras del abismo.

The Jump

Jump again, Antinous. This is your vocation.
To reveal the longing of your flesh among the stones.
Liturgy that escapes. Incomprehensible detail.
To destroy beauty.
To show the body without love. Cold-blooded.
Splashing the cliffs.
Antinous is jumping. Crashing in the depths of himself.
And we all jump with him. All the misery of not being.
All our meekness. All the disgust. All the minuscule
fits in your beautiful body, captive.
Stab the adjective. Such a stab is the pain of naming you.
Yes, when I embrace a man, I embrace the antiquity of this
    myth.
I embrace his past. I sprinkle over the beasts
the members of the future and the past.
Like that, while you jump, I'm thinking of you.
Everything jumps with you. I'm thinking of you.
I am throwing you with disastrous force,
the force of our race without destiny.
It is only jumping. As if nothing.
Like mapping new roads.
Irresponsibly desolate. Warm the gun
in the half-open mouth of the convict.
At midnight the jump.
Always the same jump in the same place.
Antinous is jumping. And we all jump with him.
Sweet, the suicides' vocation. To be devoured.
I jump with you in a succession of contingencies.
My jump is not new with the centuries.
When a man jumps, we crash with him.
We break. Scattered.
So we reach purity.
Down below are the rocks. The tempting rocks of the abyss.

El circo

Pasen. Señores. Pasen. No se detengan. Sigan.
Adéntrense hasta el fondo. Será una gran función
Verán a los lagartos rasgándose la piel. Sin
inmutarse. Verán al fin qué pasa
detrás de mis telones. Pasen. Señores. Pasen.
No se detengan. Sigan. Pobrísimo payaso
reiré para ustedes. Lloraré para ustedes.
Haré saltar los goznes y sólo para ustedes
Seré la bailarina que galopa desnuda
mostrando centelleante el arco de su pubis.
La cadera redonda. Lo erecto de sus pechos
es también para ustedes. Toda esta gran fanfarria.
Toda esta algarabía. Este andamiaje tenso de cuerdas
para ustedes. Este clown festinado lo sirvo
para ustedes. Oropel. Aderezo.
Ofrendas de primera a los leones.
Pasen señores. Pasen. No se detengan. Sigan.
Verán como transmuto en oro sus cristales.
Y trasvesti del odio daré los puntapiés con alegría.
Juro solemnemente: no será doloroso. Pero pasen.
Por Dios. ¿Qué es un circo sin público?
Sin todos los ustedes que aplauden por piedad.
Por simpatía. Por hipnosis. Por miedo.
Pasen. Que pasen todos. La carpa ya está lista.
Y listos los remiendos. Los parches del apuro.
Pasen. Señores. Pasen.
Atentos los pulgares que apunten hacia abajo.
Atentos los pulgares que apunten hacia arriba.
Verán todos sus sueños hecho añicos.
Es pura ilusión óptica. Verán cómo les robo
su pobre identidad con mi sombrero.
Cómo pagan mis liebres su tonta rebeldía.
Pasen. Señores. Pasen. No se detengan. Sigan.
Adéntrense hasta el fondo.

The Circus

Come in. *Señores*. Come in. Do not stop. Please continue.
Walk until the end. This will be a great act.
You will see lizards scraping their skin. Immutably.
Finally you will see what happens
behind my curtains. Come in. *Señores*. Come in.
Do not stop. Continue. The very poor clown,
I will laugh for you. I will cry for you.
I will make the hinges jump and only for you all
will I be the dancer that, while galloping naked,
shows the shimmering arc of her pubis.
The round hips. The erection of her breasts
are also for you. All this grand fanfare.
All this gibberish. All this tense scaffold of chords
for you. I wait on you, this accelerated clown.
Tinsel. Dressing. First-class offerings for the lions.
Come in. *Señores*. Come in. Do not stop. Continue.
You will see how I transmute your crystals into gold.
A transvestite of hatred, I will kick with happiness.
I solemnly pledge: it won't be painful. But come in.
For God's sake. What's a circus without an audience?
Without all the *yous* that applaud out of pity.
Out of sympathy. Through hypnosis. Through fear.
Come in. May everyone come in. The tent is ready.
And ready the mendings. The patches of haste.
Come in. *Señores*. Come in.
Attention, the thumbs that will point down.
Attention, the thumbs that will point up.
You will see all your dreams broken to pieces.
This is a pure optical illusion. You will see
how I steal with my hat your poor identity.
How my hares pay for their foolish rebellion.
Come in. *Señores*. Come in. Do not stop. Continue.
Walk until the end.

Un rostro en la muchedumbre

¿No ven que ando desnuda? ¿No ven que en la avalancha
abandoné mis trajes? ¿Mi sonrisa de buena cortesana?
No ven acaso que deambulo desnuda. Desdibujado el rostro.
Cosido por aplausos detrás de los carteles.
¿No ven que ya no puedo volver a los orígenes?
Flexión del tronco. A ver. Flexión de extremidades. A ver.
¿Por qué no miran? ¿Por qué no me señalan con el dedo
si me exhibo desnuda ante esta muchedumbre que ciega.
Sorda. Muda. Premia mi desnudez? ¿Es que no se dan cuenta?
¿No ven que ando desnuda? ¿Sin tregua? ¿Sin descanso?
Ahora ¿por qué me aclaman si digo estoy desnuda?
Estoy desnuda. Grito. *"Dejadme la esperanza."*
La desnuda esperanza en que me amparo.

A Face in the Crowd

Can't you see that I am walking naked? Can't you see that I
abandoned my dresses in the avalanche? My smile of the good
   courtesan?
Can't you see, at least, that I wander naked? My face erased?
Sewn by applause behind the posters?
Can't you see that I cannot return to my origins?
The torso flexed. Let's see. Extremities flexed. Let's see.
Why doesn't everybody look? Why doesn't anyone point at me
as I exhibit myself, nude, before this blind multitude
that deaf, mute, rewards my nudity? Could it be
they don't realize? Can't they see that I walk naked?
Without truce? Without rest?
Now, why do they acclaim me when I say that I am naked?
I am naked. I yell. *"Leave me hope."*
The naked hope in which I find shelter.

Variación de Helena

a Alex

La guerra desatada a mi favor apenas fue una ofrenda.
Un recurso del odio donde mi piel no estaba.
Transida. Gélida. De gasas vaporosas. Lejos. No descansé.
Gritos. Lanzas. Carruajes destrozaron mi sueño.
Ni un solo ruiseñor. Ni un solo canto. Ni una palabra grata.
Leve. Mi pálida plegaria no llegó a ningún sitio. Yo era
la desterrada. Tan sólo era mi nombre el que vagaba.
En mi nombre los hombres se mataron. Prueba de mi inocencia
era la blanca región donde imploré mil veces y maldije
mil veces al varón. A su estulticia. Al tropel de corceles.
A la sangre vertida por mi espectro. Los hombres no me oyeron.
Los hombres. Los torpes oidores sentíanse felices. Guerreaban.
Allí mi piel no estuvo. *"Yo nunca estuve en Troya. Yo
sólo fui un fantasma."*

Variation of Helen

to Alex

The war that began in my favor was but an offering.
Hatred's resource where my flesh was absent.
Wretched. Frozen. Of vaporous gauze. Afar. I didn't rest.
Screams. Spears. Carriages destroyed my dreams.
Not a nightingale. Not one chant. Nor a pleasing word.
Light. My pale prayer didn't reach any place. I was
the exiled. It was just my name that wandered.
In my name men killed themselves. Proof of my innocence,
the white region where I implored a thousand times, cursed
the male a thousand times. Cursed his foolishness. The mad rush
of chargers. The blood flowing around my image. Men did not
listen to me. Men. The foolish listeners felt happy.
They were fighting. My flesh was not there.
"I was never at Troy. I was only a ghost."

La nave de los locos

Porque ya nada sé. Porque si alguna vez supe
desecha entre las zarzas he olvidado.
Aquí duelen espinas. Aquí duelen los cardos.
Aquí dejo mi olor. Olor de perseguido.
De animal acosado por todas las jaurías bestiales del infierno.
Porque ya nada sé. Porque apenas me palpo una rodilla
y repito su nombre. Y ya no sé más nada. Y soy
esta ciudad que se derrumba. Y soy
este país de locos náufragos. Dejados en su nave a la deriva.
Porque ya nada sé. Los perros devoraron mi memoria.
¿A dónde voy? ¿A dónde vamos todos? ¿A dónde van?
¿A dónde? ¿Sabe alguien a dónde dirigirse que no sea
tan sólo a un espejismo? A ver:
¿Quién me indemniza? ¿A quién puedo condenar al destierro
por haber arruinado mi manzana? ¿La manzana de todos?
¿Cuál es Caín? ¿Y Abel? ¿Quién el bueno? ¿Y el malo?
¿Por qué tapian con hiedras mis opacas pupilas
y ya no veo más nada y ya no sé más nada?
Y si alguna vez supe
entre zarzas ardientes y jaurías sangrientas lo he olvidado.

The Ship of the Insane

Because I no longer know. Because if I once knew,
dissolving among the brambles, I have forgotten.
Here thorns that tear. Here tearing thistles.
Here I leave my scent. Scent of the persecuted.
Of an animal hunted by beasts, by the hounds from hell.
Because I no longer know. Because I can barely feel my knee,
and I repeat his name. And I know no more. And I am
this city falling down. And I am this country
of furious wrecks. Left to drift in their ship.
Because I no longer know. The dogs devoured my memory.
Where am I going? Where are all of us going?
Where are they going? Where? Does someone know
where to go that isn't a mirage? Let's see:
Who would indemnify me? Whom can I condemn to exile
for ruining my apple? Everyone's apple?
Who is Cain? Who is Abel? Who the good one? And the bad
   one?
Why are my pupils dark, why walled with ivy?
I see nothing. And I no longer know.
And if I ever knew,
between the burning brambles and the bleeding hounds, I have
   forgotten.

Elogio a la belleza

Sin flores ya. Sin fruto. Perdida la raíz y la memoria. He aquí
que ahora pretendo sucumbir al milagro violento de mi rosa.
Mi rosa cardinal. La de los vientos. Un nerviosismo púrpura
esclavo entre dos páginas.
No sé de dónde viene este clamor de cisne. No sé ni en qué
    mentir.
No sé si miento. No sé si una palabra pueda servir de enlace.
De puente que no cruzo y me traiciono. Un hombre. Un eslabón
    perdido.
Hombre que es una brecha abierta ciegamente desde el fondo.
Se hace un punto innombrable entre dos estaciones.
Esta es mi rosa. Pura deidad bicéfala. Esta otra vez mi rosa.
Serena encrucijada donde todo es posible. Todo es riesgo.
Todo salto es la vida. Laberinto perfecto.
Los finísimos hilos conducen sin piedad hacia el regreso.
Donde todo es origen. Embriones del perdón en que alimento
la afilada costumbre de mi rosa. La rosa nos condena
entre sus pétalos. Clemencia necesaria. Los óleos. El incienso.
La antorcha en las alturas ilumina el ritual. El sacrificio.
Los ojos ya no pueden seguir enamorándose en sus órbitas.
Y caen. Devorados. Y hambrientos. Y felices.
Dejándose inmolar por la belleza. Sobran los ademanes
    elocuentes.
Asistan a esta guerra desarmados. Déjense arrebatar los
    instrumentos.
No giman. No argumenten. Para qué. Contra qué defendernos.
Mis manos se resignan sobre el incauto pecho.
Magnífica virtud del abandono. De rodillas. Mujer. Ante la rosa.
Sin gloria. Sin blasones. La soledad se ahoga en el misterio.
Allí comienza el hombre. Se termina. Sostiene una batalla
brutal con la pureza. De nuevo ante la rosa. Es el comienzo. El
    fin.
Separo nuevamente su cáliz de mis dedos. Aquí estoy yo.
Allí queda la rosa. La belleza. La indestructible rosa de los
    vientos.

Eulogy to Beauty

Already without flowers. Without fruit. Lost, roots and memory.
Listen now. I try to give in to the violet miracle of a rose.
My cardinal rose. The one from the winds. A purple impatience
jailed between two pages.
I don't know where this swan clamor comes from. I don't even
    know
in what circumstance to lie. I don't know if I lie.
I don't know if a word can serve as a link. Of a bridge
I don't cross and so betray myself. A man. A lost link.
A man, an open blind breach from the depth.
Becomes a nameless point between two seasons.
This is my rose. Pure bicephalic deity. Again, my rose.
Serene crossroads where anything is possible. Every act's a risk.
Every jump is life. Perfect labyrinth.
The finest threads guide us without mercy to a returning.
Where everything is origin. Embryos of forgiveness in which I
    nourish
the sharp habits of my rose. The rose condemns us
among its petals. Necessary clemency. The unction. The incense.
The highest torch illuminates the ritual. The sacrifice.
Now eyes can no longer fall in love with their orbits.
And they fall. Devoured. Hungry. And pleased.
They let themselves immolate with beauty. The many eloquent
gestures are left behind. Come to this war unarmed.
Let them steal your instruments. Don't cry. Don't argue.
For what purpose? Against what do we defend ourselves?
My hands are resigned to my incautious chest.
Magnificent virtue the thing of abandonment.
On her knees. A woman. Before a rose.
Without glory. Without vessels. Solitude drowns in the mystery.
There, the beginning of man. And his end. A brutal battle
begins against purity. Again, before the rose. It is the beginning.
The end. I separate once more his chalice from my fingers. Here
    I am.
There, the rose. Beauty. The indestructible rose of the winds.

Arte poética de primera instancia

al poeta Benjamín Molöis, ahorcado en Sudáfrica
el 15 de octubre de 1985

Dentro de poco tiempo comenzaré mi vida en tercera
    dimensión.
Quizás dentro de un rato
me sumaré al poema más largo de la historia.
Yo no pude escoger
la pena que destila por la soga;
ellos lo decidieron.
Me van a dar un rango   un espacio antológico
me van a convertir en estandarte.
Yo sólo quería ser un poeta   humildemente vivo
medianamente anónimo
que vivir y escribir fueran en sí lo mismo.
Yo no pude escoger
qué pena se derrumba por los mástiles.
Un poeta se ahorca   por ejemplo,
cuando no se acomoda a sus designios.
A mí me van a ahorcar.
Yo no pude escoger el gajo resistente de las culpas
ni el color de mi piel.
Ellos lo decidieron.

Juro que no fui yo quien se propuso
borrar las limitantes del idioma.
Yo no pude escoger de qué modo posar
ni el traje de lucir a los efectos.
Ellos lo decidieron.
Sé que dentro de un rato millares de poetas
perderán el aliento aunque sea un minuto;
trascenderé las lenguas y los espumarajos
habrá declaraciones y protestas.
Yo no pude escoger.
Yo sólo era   un poeta rebelde
casi enemigo de la inmortalidad.

Poetic Art of the First Instance

to the poet Benjamín Molöis, hanged
in South Africa on October 15, 1985

Soon my life will start its third dimension.
Perhaps very soon
I will add myself to the longest poem in history.
I could not choose
the sorrow that trickles down the rope.
They made the decision.
They are giving me a rank   a space in an anthology
they are making a standard out of me.
I only wanted to be a poet   humbly alive
half anonymous
where living and writing would in fact be the same.
I could not choose
the sorrow tumbling down the post.
A poet hangs himself   for example
when he cannot conform to his own design.
But they are going to hang me.
I could not choose the branch most resistant to guilt
nor the color of my skin. They decided it.

I swear I wasn't the one who wanted to erase
the limits of language.
I could not choose which way to pose
nor the clothes to wear for the best effect.
They decided it.
I know that very soon thousands of poets
will stop breathing if just for a minute;
I will transcend language and diminutives.
There will be declarations, protests.
I could not choose.
I was just   a rebel poet
almost the enemy of immortality.

Perdonen que no pueda tutearlos   camaradas.
No estaba en mi intención la trascendencia.
Yo no pude escoger ni mi piel ni mi muerte
y menos   la ascensión.
Ellos lo decidieron
y no se equivocaron.

Forgive me that I cannot treat you as equals,   *camaradas*.
It wasn't my intention to rise.
I could not choose my skin or my death
much less   my ascension.
They decided it
and they were not misled.

Los 400 golpes

Culpable. No era el perdón. Era el olvido
lo que entraba a raudales.
Culpable. Un martillazo. Y otro martillazo.
Y luego otro. Y otro.
Tristísimo golpear en resonancias.

Culpable.
Alguien habla en tono mayor de la benevolencia.
Empuña con destreza el bastón de la ternura.
Apunta al corazón.
Que no falle ese golpe delicado y certero.

Culpable.
El ojo registra
en imágenes perfectas
la sagrada bondad del asesino.

Culpable.
Un martillazo. Y otro martillazo.
Y duro contra el pecho. Y duro contra el órgano.
Es el castigo.
La piedad será si acaso sobrevive.

Guilty. It was not the forgiveness. But the forgetting
coming in torrents.
Guilty. A hammer blow. And another hammer blow.
And then another. And another.
So sad, this rhythmic resonance.

Guilty.
Someone speaks in a major key about benevolence.
Skillfully grasps the cane of tenderness.
Points to the heart.
That delicate, certain blow must not fail.

Guilty.
The eye registers
the perfect images,
the murderer's sacred goodness.

Guilty.
A hammer blow. And another hammer blow.
And hard against the chest. And hard against the organ.
This is the punishment.
There will be mercy, but only on survival.

La hora de la estrella

Para que yo naciera mi madre hizo un montón
feroz con sus andrajos. Entre trama y urdidumbre
me fue tejiendo a tientas. Violenta sobre el piso
lloró mi nacimiento. Mi muerte. El nacimiento y muerte
de mis hijos. Y se supo culpable. Mi madre era culpable
del hombre que escupió su prójimo en mi entraña.
Por eso se desgarra sobre su propia estirpe.
Y yo le grito: Madre. Madre. ¡Por Dios! Pero no acude nadie.
Mi madre está de espaldas. Revuelta entre sus trapos.
Se aleja. Prisionera de sus ripios. Sus ojos
están húmedos. Mi madre se desliza en dos por sus mejillas.
A lo lejos sus brazos son un vago ademán.
Firman un veredicto. Mi madre se me escurre
líquida entre los dedos. Se esfuma agonizante.
Se pierde con el siglo.

The Hour of the Star

For me to be born, my mother made of her rags
a fierce mountain. Between scheme and intrigue she wove me
while groping in the dark. Violently against the floor
she cried out my birth. My death. The births and deaths
of my children. She knew herself guilty. My mother,
guilty of the man who spit mankind into my womb.
She rends herself on her bloodline.
And I yell at her: Mother. Mother. For God's sake!
But no one comes. My mother's back is turned.
Shrouded in torn clothes. She goes away.
Prisoner of her own debris. Her eyes,
humid. My mother slides in two down her cheeks.
From afar, her arms are a vague token.
They sign a verdict. My mother trickles away
liquid through my fingers. She vanishes agonizing.
She loses herself with the century.

Plegaria contra el miedo

Volando está la voz. Su frágil marioneta con hilos invisibles.
Finísimas agujas hilvanan dulcemente un tenue claro-oscuro
sobre el mantel del tiempo. Del tiempo que nos deja.
Que nos levanta en vilo. Que a veces. Por azar.
Nos multiplica. Lenta. Muy lenta. Leve. Miro a mi alrededor.
Entono esta plegaria contra el miedo. Contra el miedo
del hombre que se arrastra. Silba. Vuelve a escupir. Maldice.
Vuelve a escupir. Alaba. Se duele. Me lastima. Se dobla.
Me desplaza. Contra ti mi plegaria. Plegaria contra el miedo.
Mezcla de horror y júbilo. De fibra lacerada.
Contra mi lado oculto. Contra las aguas mansas. Contra ti.
Contra todo. La voz. La voz. Su frágil marioneta.
La débil manecilla pendiente de la voz. La voz sobre su eje.
Aquí dejo el renglón en mansedumbre.
Aquí será la voz. Lenta. Muy lentamente. Lenta aclama la voz.
Se torna rictus. Regresa a los nostálgicos colores.
Imploran los que fuimos tan muertos por el fuego
y volvemos llorando al ojo de agua.

A Prayer Against Fear

The voice is flying. Its frail marionette with invisible threads.
The finest needles baste sweetly a tenuous chiaroscuro
over the mantle of time. Of the time that leaves us.
Wakes us in suspense. That sometimes. By luck.
Multiplies us. Slowly. Very slowly. Lightly. I look around me.
I intone this prayer against fear. Against the fear
of the man that creeps. Whistles. Spits again. Curses.
Spits again. Praises. Is hurt. Hurts me. Folds himself.
Displaces me. Against you I pray. A prayer against fear.
Both pain and joy. Lacerated fiber.
Against my darkest side. Against gentle water.
Against you. Against everything.
The voice. The voice. The frail marionette.
The frail watch hand expecting the voice. The voice
over its axle. Here I leave the line tame.
Here the voice will be. Slowly. Very slowly. Slowly the voice
acclaims. It turns a rictus. It returns to nostalgic colors.
Those of us killed by fire
are imploring, and crying we return to the spring.

La trampa

No obstante, sólo puedo alegar a mi favor
que a veces cedo. Caigo en minúsculas trampas
que nos arma la vida. En trampas como jaulas
para cazar gorriones. En delicadas trampas.
Que algunos días. ¡Oh, días específicos!
al abrir el balcón. Al asomarme y ver
con todos los sentidos. Y oír con todos los sentidos.
Y oler con todos los sentidos. Soy un terco violín
en evidencia. A veces — excusa delirante —
la vida se me vira como un juego de cartas
mostrádome los triunfos.
Me enamora con labios nuevecitos. Me apremia,
imprescindible, un cuarto movimiento.
Novena Sinfonía de Ludwig Van Beethoven.
Como una credencial. Un aquí está mi mano.
Mis millones de manos.
La piel se me estremece de piedad infinita:
El hombre mata. Muere. Miente. Roba. Claudica
de espaldas a esa música en un afán voraz de permanencia.
Confunde libertad con desplazarse.
El hombre duerme armado contra los otros hombres
y contra el hombrecito
que habita los rincones más claros de su pecho.
A pesar de esa música. A pesar del balcón.
Del sol que estreno. A pesar de esa Oda feroz
a la alegría. De la limpia mañana
que niega los despojos de la cena de ayer.
No obstante. Digo. La vida hoy se presenta como un traje.
Y sé que es una trampa. Pero cedo. Y me dejo embriagar.
Y acepto cualquier tregua. Y soy un espiral.
Un balancín. Un coro. Porque sucede a veces
que al abrir el balcón. Al asomarme y ver.
Y oír. Y oler. Con todos los sentidos.
La vida me ha sacado barajas de la manga.
No obstante, sólo puedo alegar a mi favor:
es una trampa. Y me dejo caer.

The Trap

Nevertheless, I can only say on my behalf
that sometimes I give up. I fall into little traps
that life rigs up for us. In traps like cages
for catching sparrows. Inside delicate traps,
on some days. Oh, specific days!
I open the balcony, I glimpse, I see
with all my senses. I listen with all my senses.
Smell with all my senses. I am a stubborn violin,
a witness. And sometimes — delirious excuse —
my life turns into a card game
and shows me triumphs.
It seduces me with new lips. Rewards me,
indispensably, the fourth movement,
Ninth Symphony by Ludwig Van Beethoven.
Like a credential. A here is my hand.
My millions of hands.
And my skin shudders from infinite pity:
Man kills. Dies. Lies. Steals. Gives up,
turns his back on that music with its hunger
for permanency. He who confuses liberty with displacement.
The man who sleeps armed against other men
and against the little man
who inhabits the lightest corners of his chest.
In spite of that music. In spite of the balcony.
Of the sun I inaugurate. In spite of that ferocious
Ode to happiness. That clean morning
forgetting the crumbs of yesterday.
Nevertheless. I say. Today life is a dress.
And I know it's a trap. But I give up. And I get myself drun
And accept any truce. And I am a spiral.
A balance beam. A chorus. Because, as it happens, somet
when I open the balcony. While glimpsing, looking.
And listening. And smelling. With all my senses,
life takes cards out of my sleeve.
Nevertheless, I can only say on my behalf
it's a trap. And I let myself fall.

Canción de amor para tiempos difíciles

Antonio
cuánto me dueles siendo hombre.
—ALBIS TORREZ

Difícil escribir te quiero con locura.
Hasta la misma médula. ¿Qué será de mi cuerpo
si se pierden tus manos? ¿Qué será de mis manos
si se pierde tu pelo? Difícil. Muy difícil
un poema de amor en estos tiempos.
Resulta que tú estás. Feroz en tu evidencia.
Resulta que yo estoy. Contrahecha. Acechante.
Y resulta que estamos. La ley de gravedad no nos perdona.
Difícil es decirte te quiero en estos tiempos.
Te quiero con urgencia.
Quiero hacer un aparte. Sin dudas. Y sin trampas.
Para decir te quiero. Así. Sencillamente.
Y que tu amor me salva del aullido nocturno
cuando loba demente la fiebre me arrebata.
No quiero que me duela la falta de ternura.
Pero amor. Qué difícil escribir que te quiero.
Así. *"Entre tanto gris. Tanta corcova junta."*
Cómo puedo aspirar la transparencia.
Retomar esta voz tan desgastada.
Esta costumbre antigua para decir te quiero.
Así. Sencillamente. Antiguamente. Digo.
Si todo es tan difícil. Si duele tanto todo.
Si un hombre. Y otro hombre. Y luego otro. Y otro.
Destrozan los espacios donde el amor se guarda.
Si no fuera difícil. Difícil y tremendo.
Si no fuera imposible olvidar esta rabia.
Mi reloj. Su tic-tac. La ruta hacia el cadalso.
Mi sentencia ridícula con esta cuerda falsa.
Si no fuera difícil. Difícil y tremendo.
Plasmaría este verso con su cadencia cursi.
Si fuera así de simple escribir que te quiero.

Love Song for Difficult Times

Antonio
how much it hurts being a man.
—ALBIS TORREZ

So hard to say I love you madly.
Until I reach my marrow. What would happen to my body
if I lose your hands? What would happen to my hands
if your hair is lost? So hard. Very hard
a love poem on these days.
It happens that you exist. Ferocious in your evidence.
It happens that I exist. Counterfeited. Insisting.
And it happens that we exist. The law of gravity doesn't forgive
  us.
So hard to say I love you these days.
I love you with urgency. I want to make a statement.
Without doubts. And without traps.
To say I love you. Like that. Plainly.
And that our love shall save me from the nocturnal howl
when, like a maddened she-wolf, the fever will grab me.
I don't want to be hurt by the absence of tenderness.
But love. So hard to write that I love you.
Like this. *"Between so much gray, so many hunchbacks together."*
How can I aspire to transparency.
To retake this worn-out voice.
This ancient custom of saying I love you.
Like this. Plainly. Anciently. I say.
If everything is so hard. If everything hurts so much.
If one man. And another man. And again another. And another.
Destroy the spaces where love is kept.
If it weren't hard. Hard and tremendous.
If it weren't impossible to forget this rage.
My clock. Its tick-tock. The route to the scaffold.
My ridiculous sentence with this false cord.
If it weren't hard. Hard and tremendous.
I would cast this verse with its cheap cadence.
If it were this simple to write that I love you.

Declinaciones

¿Saben que detestaba nombrar el corazón en los poemas
y el corazón castiga si lo excluyen?

Hoy más que nunca muestro claras declinaciones.
Con votos de humildad. Con una voz suavísima.
Con un leve susurro escalo el escenario.
Con un golpe de efecto descubro mis flaquezas:

Hay entre ustedes, tiernos amantes míos,
alguno que se atreva y apriete hasta la asfixia
la cincha, los arreos de la bestia.
Le acomode la carga. Le palmee los ijares.
Y le diga camina.
No escuches los silbidos siniestros del barranco.

Declinations

Did you know that I detested naming the heart in my poems
and that the heart punishes if it finds itself excluded?

Today, more than ever, I show clear declinations.
With humble vows. With a soft voice.
With a light whisper, I scale the stage.
With a stroke for effect I discover my weakness:

Is there among you, my tender lovers,
one who dares to tighten, until breathless,
the cinch, the trappings of the beast.
Dares accommodate its load. Slaps its flanks.
And commands, walk.
Don't you listen to the sinister whistles of the gorge.

El ángel exterminador

Aquí está lo terrible. Lo hermoso abrumador. Lo destructivo.
El ángel que me roza. Aro de luz. Presencia del candor que nos
    fulmina
el arquero suspenso entre dos rayos. Soy infeliz. Mortal.
Debajo de la máscara sospecho las hondísimas traiciones de mi
    cuerpo.
Me inicio en lo terrible. Iluminándome.
Las otras que soy no me determinan. Puesto que
todo ángel anuncia el exterminio. Me aferro a los maderos.
Los dejo lacerar mi pobre espalda. Arrástrense mis pies.
Es mi vía crucis. Un paso más. Un paso a la antesala del infierno.
Cómo dejar pasar las caricias mordaces de la lumbre.
Y cómo no adorar al cuerpo por el cuerpo. Al hombre en sí.
Al junco vibratorio. Variaciones del acto en que me elevo.
Fatalidad de acróbata. Lo bello. Lo terrible.
Lo insoportable eterno exhala sus burbujas. Que débil soplo soy.
Tan implorante. Hundiéndome en el cuerpo por el cuerpo.
Tratando de escapar. Y no hay salida.
Se vislumbran los restos de antiguos esplendores.
Quizás no haya más luz. Tal vez no habrá más fuego.
Quizás vuelva al país de las nieves perpetuas.
A mi disfraz de huérfana en invierno. Un ángel en la jarcia.
Acorde sigiloso de pobre aeda ciego.
Dispuesto a ejecutar mis inmundicias.
Patentizar mis actos. Mis terrores inéditos.
Un ángel es la fragua. Temedle a la belleza.
En ella se concentran la levedad y el peso.
Aquí está lo terrible. Lo hermoso destructor.
Y apenas sé si puedo soportarlo.

The Exterminating Angel

Here, the terrible thing. The beauty that overwhelms.

The destructive thing. The angel that rubs me.

Enlightened ring. Pure white presence that the astonished archer hurls at us between two lightning bolts. I am unhappy. Mortal.

I suspect the profound treason under the mask of my body.

I initiate myself into what is terrible. I shine.

The other women that I am do not determine me. Because

every angel announces extermination. I cling to the beams.

I let them lacerate my poor back. Feet of mine: crawl.

This is my Via Crucis. Another step. A step to the vestibule of hell.

How to let pass the tender pungent caresses of fire.

And how can I not adore the body for the body itself. The man himself.

The vibrating bulrush. Variations of that act in which I am elevated.

Acrobatic fatality. What is beautiful. What is terrible.

The unbearable eternity exhales its bubbles. For I am but a weak breath of air.

So imploring. Going down in the body for the body.

Trying to escape. But there is no way out.

A glimpse of the remnants from the old splendors appear.

Perhaps there will be no more light. Maybe no more fire.

Perhaps I will return to the country of eternal snow.

To my orphaned costume of winter. An angel in the medley.

Careful accord from a poor blinded bard.

Ready to recite my filth.

To patent my acts. My unpublished terrors.

An angel is the forge. Have fear of beauty.

It is concentrated lightness and weight.

Here, the terrible thing. The beauty that destroys.

I barely know if I can endure it.

Oración

Daño es esta oración y su monotonía abrumando en el vientre.
La campana. Tan lúgubre. Tan nítida. Tan sola.
Santificada sea.
Santificada sea y bendecida esta oración y el daño.
Esta oración. La gracia. El macabro ritual de los excomulgados.
Santificados sean.
Hoguera en la que danzan besándose los ruedos
santos inquisidores. Santificados sean.

Así como el olvido es una piedra. La piedra es el dolor.
No se detiene. Nunca.
Partícula de arena en el ojo de Dios.

Santificados sean en nombre de este nombre la maldición.
La rabia. La loba. La inmundicia. La cuerda. Los maderos.
El óxido. Los clavos. El daño. La campana. Su tan. Tan. Tan.
Tan inválido y triste. Santificado sea.

Prayer

Damage is this prayer and its monotony overpowering my womb.
The bell. Mournful. Exact. Lonely.
Hallowed be.
Hallowed and blessed be this prayer and this damage.
This prayer. Grace. The macabre rite of the excommunicated.
Hallowed be.
Bonfire where the inquisitors are dancing while it is kissing
their skirt hem. Hallowed be they.

Likewise, forgetting is like rock. The rock is pain.
It doesn't stop. Never.
Sand particle in the eye of God.

The curse: Hallowed be they in the name of this name.
The rage. The she-wolf. Filth. The cord. The wooden beams.
The oxide. The nails. The damage. The bell. Its tan. Tan. Tan.
So crippled and sad. Hallowed be.

El muro

a Virginia Woolf

Al Este. Al Noroeste. Desmesurado. Abrupto. Inabarcable.
Hoja de doble filo del suelo al cielo el muro.
Y una mujer delante. Debatiéndose.
Las rocas se disputan la herencia de sus sedas.
El ripio de sus trajes. Y ese dolor
reptando en las costillas. La espada y su inocencia
dibujan una zanja de hiel sobre la carne. La mujer.
Y la espada. Y el muro. Y el barranco. Y las sedas.
Y el barro. A sus pies está el cántaro. Deshecho
por los viajes a la fuente. La fuente que está seca
por toda la locura de sus lunas. Al Norte. Al Sur.
El muro. El muro y su silencio imperturbable.
Su seguro silencio alimento de yedras. La mujer
y sus ropas trizadas por el viaje. A sus ojos el muro.
A su espalda la espada. A sus pies el barranco.
Imposible avanzar. Retroceder. Imposible
arrojarse de costado. Una mirada al cielo.
Azul desentendido. La mujer debatiéndose. La mujer
y su espada. La mujer y su muro. La mujer.
Su barranco y sus zapatos rotos. Y su cara crispada
decidiendo el vacío. Un salto. Un punto. El muro.
La mudez. Y la nada.

The Wall

to Virginia Woolf

To the East. To the Northwest. Unrestrained.
Sudden. Unencompassed. Double-edged blade
from the earth to the sky, the wall.
And a woman in front. Struggling.
The rocks are arguing over her silk inheritance,
the pieces of her clothes. And that pain crawling
in her ribs. The sword in its innocence
draws a trench of gall over the skin. The woman.
And the sword. And the wall. And the cliff, the silk,
the clay, the pitcher in pieces under her feet
on the way to the fountain. And the fountain is dry
because of the insanity of its moons. To the North. To the South.
The wall. The wall and its undisturbed silence.
Its secure silence is food for the ivy. The woman
and her clothing shredded by the journey. Before her eyes, the
     wall.
At her back, the blade. At her feet, the cliff.
Impossible to go faster. To go back. Impossible
to throw one's self aside. A glance at the sky.
Heedless blue. The woman struggling, the woman
and her blade. The woman and her wall. The woman.
Her cliff and her shabby shoes. And her twitching face
deciding the emptiness. A jump. A point. The wall.
Mute. And nothing.

Autorretrato con la oreja cortada

Amaneció. Otra vez. La vida está obligando. Obligándonos.
Amaneció. Otra vez. Disuelta en el discurso. Hecha girones
por la caída anterior al vacío.
El temible vació. Devorándonos.
Vengo de todo el mal con mis reliquias.
Una oreja de menos. Y sangrante. Un disparo en la sien.
El abandono. El ridículo cuarto de un hotel miserable.
Afuera estaba el mundo. La fiesta de los otros.
Yo lo espiaba. Hambriento el ojo clavado en las hendijas.
Vengo de todo el mal.
De recorrer los círculos tortuosos del infierno.
Vengo de todo el mal; así no más: del mal.
Pero amanece. Amanece otra vez. Obligando. Obligándonos.

Self-Portrait with a Cut Ear

It's dawn. Again. Life is obliging. Obliging us.
It's dawn. Again. Dissolved in speech. Locked
in a spiral down to the last fall,
fall into nothing, horror of nothing. Devouring us.
I come with my relics of all that is wrong.
With one ear gone. And bleeding. A bullet in my temple.
Abandonment. Ridiculous bedroom of a miserable hotel.
The world was standing outside. A party of others.
I spied on them. Hungry eye nailed to openings.
I come from all that is wrong.
I travel from the torturous circles of hell.
I come from what is wrong; just that: from the wrong.
But it's dawn. It's dawn again. Obliging. Obliging us.

Devocionario

Cuchillas abundando en las pupilas.
Azul merodeador de los ribazos. Era bueno ser buenos.
Contemplarlo. Subir. Bajar. Aparte
la tristeza ante lo eterno. Aparte
la alegría con su tránsito. El mar. Estar y ser.
Dosificados. Mínimos. Calientes. Emerger. Sumergir.
El mar y su cadencia. Salivazo de sal sobre tu rostro.
Atropello del límite era el mar contra este verso roto.
Cristales descompuestos del ritmo en la marea.
Abajo el mar. Arriba era el mar en el mar. Y era
la angustia dolorosa del yodo. Era empuñar la vasta
superficie del mar a través de la carne. Afuera. Adentro.
Canción de intensidad. Madero desolado. El cuerpo
bajo el cuerpo. El mar encima. Afuera. Adentro.
A un lado. También al otro lado. Húmeda la oquedad.
Liviana la osamenta. El pecho atormentado. El mar.
Despacio. Suave. Quebrándonos por siempre. Desde siempre.
Añicos los espejos. Aletazos del mar entre los párpados.

In her eyes, knife-thrusts galore.
Plundering blue of mounds. It was good to be good.
To gaze at it all. Go up. Go down. Aside,
sadness before eternity. Aside,
happiness on its journey. The ocean. To exist and be.
Measured. Minimal. Hot. Surface. Submerge.
The ocean and its cadence. Spit of salt on your face.
An assault of the limits was the ocean against this broken verse.
Rhythm's decomposed crystals in the tide.
Below, the sea. Above, the sea within the sea. And it was
iodine's true anguish. It was wielding the huge
ocean surfaces through the skin. Outside. Inside.
Earsplitting song. Desolate beam. The body
under the body. The ocean above. Outside. Inside.
To one side. And to the other, too. Humid, the cavity.
Light, the bones. The chest in torment. The ocean.
Slowly. Easy. Breaking us for all time. Since all time.
The mirrors in bits. Ocean flutters between the eyelids.

Razones del diluvio

¡Ay, qué pena me das, Esperanza, por Dios!
Cinco treinta minutos en todos los relojes de esta tarde
en que empiezo a llover. Por recurrencia.
Sólo porque desfilan temblores en mis hojas.
Y soy un instrumento. Me abandono.
Me dejo adormecer. Uno tras otro acuden
enlodados fantasmas. Empolvados fantasmas.
Reclaman oraciones desmedidas.
¡Ay, qué pena me das, Esperanza, por Dios!
Podrida la raíz y ya sin frutos
el árbol que talaron en tu nombre.
Se rompió el quinto sello:
cinco treinta minutos en todos los relojes de esta tarde.
Continúo lloviendo a borbotones.
Oigo cómo se extienden nostalgias sobre el musgo.
Me da pena. Por Dios que me da pena tu escudo pequeñísimo.
Que ya casi no sirve para ocultar tus partes vulnerables.
Ay, qué pena me das, Esperanza sin Dios.
¡Esperanza sin nadie! Te agotaron.
Cinco treinta minutos en todos los relojes de la tarde.

Reasons for the Flood

Ay, what sadness you cause me, Esperanza, for God's sake!
Five-thirty on all the clocks of the afternoon
in which I start to rain. Through appeals.
Only because temblors are marching on my leaves.
And I am an instrument. I abandon myself.
I let myself sleep. The muddy ghosts come
one after another. Powdered ghosts.
They're greedy for prayers.
Ay, what sadness you cause me, Esperanza, for God's sake!
Rotten the roots and already without fruit
the tree that was pruned in your name.
The fifth seal is broken:
Five-thirty on all the clocks of the afternoon.
I continue to rain in torrents.
I hear nostalgias extending over moss.
I feel sorry. I swear to God that I feel sorry for your little shield.
It is almost no longer enough to cover your vulnerable parts.
Ay, what sadness you cause me, *Esperanza* without God.
Esperanza without anyone! They drained you.
Five-thirty on all the clocks of the afternoon.

Ora Pro Nobis

Mis bienamados muertos. Mis amantes.
Las manchas de sus cuerpos en mis cuerpos.
Mis cuerpos sucesivos sucediéndose
en pactos que firmamos contra toda cordura.
Mis bienamados muertos. Mis muertos escabrosos.
De cada pulsación resulta un latigazo.
Blanda espina dorsal. Miércoles de ceniza.
Herreros doblegados sobre el yunque
nos moldearon con fuego. Al rojo vivo.
Nos quemaron la carne. La memoria.
Y nos dieron un nombre. Una cerca. Un cordel.
Un espacio habitat donde alinearnos
haciéndonos marchar en fila india.
Mis bienamados muertos. Mis resúmenes.
Mis muertos que se agobian y me agobian
con el exacto peso de sus tibias. Sus iniciales rotas.
Sus órdenes simbólicos en la cronología. Manos.
Manos. Manos y bocas. Manos crispadas. Yertas.
Las palmas hacia arriba.
Las bocas implorando lugar en los recuerdos.
Cada vez menos yo. Cada vez más disuelta en aguas ocasionales.
Cada vez más borrosa silueta en las barajas.
Mis pobres buenos muertos. Mis muertos enmendados en la
    prisa.
Aquí estoy. Como siempre.
De afuera llegan ruidos. Fragmentos de oraciones fugitivas.
La noche larga corre tras de sí sus pestillos.
Largamente aullaré con mi agonía.
Mis bienamados muertos. Amantes mustios. Torpes.
Sus cuerpos y mis cuerpos en muertes sucesivas.

Ora Pro Nobis

My dearly beloved dead. My lovers.
The taint of your bodies on my body.
My successive body happening
in alliances we signed against all judgment.
My dearly beloved dead. My scabrous dead.
From each pulse a lash is growing.
Soft dorsal spine. Ash Wednesday.
Brandished smiths over the anvil
molded us with fire. At the living red.
They burned our skin. Our memory.
And they gave us a name. A fence. A string.
A habitat, a space in which they lined us up,
made us march straight.
My dearly beloved dead. My summaries.
My dead ones who exhaust themselves and exhaust me
with the exact weight of their shinbones. Their broken initials.
Their symbolic order in chronology. Hands.
Hands. Hands and mouths. Closed hands. Stiffened.
Palms up.
Their mouths imploring a place in memory.
Each time I become less me. Each time I dissolve
more in the occasional waters. Each time the more
faded silhouette on the cards.
My poor beloved. My dead ones mended in a hurry.
Here I am. As always.
I hear noises from the outside. Fragments of fugitive sentences.
The long night locks its bolts.
I will howl long in my agony.
My dearly beloved dead. Faded lovers. Foolish lovers.
Their bodies and my bodies in a succession of deaths.

Dies Irae

El ojo es el paisaje que sobre él se cierne. Acorralándolo.
Rota la antigua alianza revelo agonizante
que el paisaje es redondo. Que redondo es el ojo. Que saberlo
no salva de tanta inmensidad indiferente.
Mis hijos amputaron sus embriones. Decidieron crecer
entre el azar y el miedo con sus prerrogativas.
Casuales ellos mismos descubren que están solos. Saltan.
Se quiebran. Gritan. Y mi vientre se espanta
ante la gran pupila tumefacta del cíclope.
¡Ay, Ulises, cuánto nos cuesta este regreso a Itaca!
¡Cuántos cuerpos dolientes
pudriéndose en nombre de la sobrevivencia!

Mis hijos van buscando su isla en mis rincones. Cortan.
Destazan. Tiemblan. Buscan en mí el paisaje
redondo para el ojo. El ojo es el paisaje. Saberlo
no nos salva del punzante atentado. De la afilada lanza.
¡Ay, Ulises, cuánta ceguera cuesta esta arena blanquísima!
¡Cuánta cuenca vacía!
¡Cuánto cadáver triste meciéndose en la playa!
Cuánto. ¡Cuánto nos duele este regreso a Itaca!

Dies Irae

The eye is scenery that blossoms over itself. Trapping itself.
Broken, the old alliance. I deadly reveal
that the scenery is round, the eye round. That knowing this
does not save us from such indifferent immensity.
My children amputated their embryos. Between luck, fear,
and their prerogatives, they decided to grow.
Casually they discover, themselves, that they are alone. They
    jump.
They break. They scream. And my womb halts, fearful
before the grand swollen eye of the cyclops.
Ay, Ulysses, how much it has cost, this return to Ithaca!
How many painful bodies turning
putrid in the name of survival!

My children are searching for the island
in the corners of my body. They cut. They slice.
They tremble. They search in me for the round scenery,
for the eye. The eye is the scenery. Knowing this
does not save us from the assault. From the sharpened spear.
Ay, Ulysses, how much blindness has this pure white sand cost
    us!
How empty the sockets!
How many sad corpses swinging on the beach!
How much. How much it hurts to return to Ithaca!

Lamento por Frida Kahlo

Yo no sé. No imagino siquiera cómo duele. Cómo gime la piel.
Cómo se rasga. Yo no sé. Yo no sé. No sé de este alarido
brutal que te encadena al alto respaldar de los sillones.
A mí sólo llegaste fragmento de vasija. Costilla de alfarero.
Sabor ajeno el barro sobre la lengua mansa.
Invocación salobre de los oscuros pájaros.
Cántaro a donde acudo con largas letanías. Largas horas.
Largos surcos de lágrimas. Yo no sé.
Yo no sé. Yo no sé hacer saltar destellos que deliren.
No imagino arlequines que vagamente asistan al ocaso.
Yo no sé. Yo no sé cómo duele. Yo estoy aquí. Postrándome.
En otra dimensión.
Esclava en los rigores de otras leyes.

Lament for Frida Kahlo

I don't know. I can't even imagine how it hurts. How the skin
   moans.
How it rips itself. I don't know. I don't know. I don't know about
this brutal howl that chains you to the high backs of chairs.
To me you came as a vessel fragment. Rib of a potter.
Foreign taste, clay over the meek tongue.
Salty invocation of dark birds.
Clay pot where I too run with my long litanies. Long hours.
Long furrows of tears. I don't know.
I don't know. I don't know how to make the sparks jump in
   delirium.
I can't imagine harlequins lazily attending to the sunset.
I don't know how it hurts. I am here. Kneeling down.
In another dimension.
Slave to the rigors of other laws.

Si yo pudiera estar

a Juan José Dalton

Ay, padre,
si usted pudiera verme este día o cualquiera.
Si usted pudiera ver mi huella en su calzado
emparentando el polvo, la cruz, la contramarcha.
Si usted pudiera estar en mi estatura púdica.

Ay, padre que acompaño del terror de la infancia
que muy a su pesar entra en mis estaciones
era tan importante no transcurrir de espaldas
que dividí el insomnio
el ríspido bautizo sobre las cicatrices
sobre lo que no entiendo
o mal entiendo siempre.
Si yo pudiera abrirle mi espacio en la andanada
y el riesgo necesario de las primeras filas
darle como argumento la furia y los obstáculos
que arrasan los volcanes.
Si no hubiera crecido tan hijo de su sexo
estaría perpetuo sentado en sus rodillas
pequeño
perdido en mi destierro.

If I Could Be

to Juan José Dalton

Ay, father,
if you could see me today or any other day,
if you could see my footprint in your shoeprint
making a family with the dust, the cross,
the countermarch.
If you were only my chaste height.

Ay, father, who I accompany from the terror of my infancy,
who, though sorry, enters my seasons.
It was so important not to pass by you with my back turned
that I divided my insomnia
like a rough baptism over the scars
of what I do not understand
or misunderstood always.
If I could give him my place in the grandstands
and the necessary risk of the front lines,
offer him, as argument, the fury and the obstacles
that raze volcanos.
If I hadn't grown so entirely into the son of his sex
I might yet be seated on his knee
little
lost in my exile.

No pude ser el mar

mamá

Ayúdame otra vez a resolver la vida.
Tengo miedo a los pequeños insectos que me habitan
y anuncian
la hora de los solos.

Donde te miro, hay una soledad como los parques.

Enséñame a entender que ya crecí
que mis juguetes alcanzan otra altura
y debo ser exacta.

Tú no tienes la culpa
de que mi angustia tenga tus manos apuradas
tu mala manera de decir:
estás acabando con mi vida.

Pero ya no es tu vida la que acabo
es la mía la que rompo contra los arrecifes
porque nunca olvidé que quise ser el mar
y no tuve las aguas suficientes.

Todos pagamos nuestra cuota de nuncas
yo no lo supe
hasta que tropecé con la intemperie.
Llevo sobre la espalda el paquete redondo
que me diste diciendo:
Es el Mundo

y no me atrevo a abrirlo porque suena a reloj.

Discúlpame esta hora de flaquezas
y descorazonamientos:
estoy desnuda
cargada de presagios.

I Could Not Be the Sea

mamá

Help me again to resolve my life.
I'm afraid of the small insects that inhabit me
and announce
the hour of the lonely ones.

Where I look at you there is solitude, as in parks.

Teach me to understand that I have already grown,
that my toys reach other heights,
and that I should be exact.

You are not the one to blame
for my anguish that hurries your hands,
not the one to blame for your bad way of saying,
you are finishing with my life.

But it is not your life I am finishing.
It's my own I break against the reefs
because I never forgot that I wanted to be the sea
and there wasn't enough waters.

We all pay for our share of nevers.
I didn't know
until I stumbled against the open air.
I carry on my back the round pack
you gave me, saying:
It's the World

and I dare not open it, for it ticks like a clock.

Forgive me this hour of weakness
and dejection.
I'm naked,
charged with premonitions.

Retrato adolescente

Entonces yo sabía quién era el mal
separado del bien por una línea tenue
indefinida
todo era claro y firme:
desayunar, crecer
clavada entre la nuez
y sus antípodas.
Mi madre era el estado con sus leyes
mi padre era la masa reprimida
el orden era el orden
yo era sólo una niña que entrenaba
para futuras várices y estrías.

Todo era claro y firme:
obedecer, callar
no tengas vocación de oveja negra.

Ahora, en qué estante del orden aprendido
guardo la heterodoxia, si no alcanzo a entender
cuándo decomisaron mis bromas de muchacha.

Adolescent Portrait

Then I knew who was evil,
separated from good by a delicate line,
undefined,
everything clear and firm:
eat breakfast, grow,
nailed to the nut
and its antipodes.
My mother was the state with its laws,
my father the repressed masses.
Order was order.
I was only a little girl in training
for future varicose veins and stretch marks.

Everything was clear and firm:
obey stay quiet
don't have the vocation of a black sheep.

Now, on what level of the order learned
do I keep my disbelief if I cannot come to an understanding
when my girlish play was confiscated.

Lloremos y seamos felices

Ah, mi amigo, el innombrable
acabamos de inaugurar la entrada del invierno
qué turbio el hijo pródigo
qué ruinas bien vestidas
para esconder la lobreguez remota de los castos.

Ah, mi amigo, se nos pierde la esfera
qué deshilvan se suelta en la ternura
qué tiempo tan vivido descompone
la incertidumbre misma.
Qué haremos del pronóstico y los advenedizos
a dónde fue a parar la pulcritud del pasto.

Ah, mi amigo, del siempre quizás nunca
recibimos compactos
la irrupción del invierno
y cada vez más verdes las alucinaciones
cada vez más videntes de esta Era
que nos desorganiza y reconstruye.
¡Hay tanto por hacer
y tan poco hemos hecho!
Lloremos, y además, seamos felices
felices de no ser
de lo que fuimos
de los quizás seremos.

Ah, mi amigo, desde el arco voltaico
si lo más importante
es que, ni usted ni yo somos
tan importantes como esta novedad.

Ah, mi amigo, el bienaventurado
lloremos otra vez
y seamos felices.

Let's Cry and Be Happy

Ah, mi amigo, unnameable,
we have finished inaugurating winter's entrance.
How turbid, the prodigal son.
What ruins, and so well dressed they are
for hiding the sadness of the chaste.

Ah, mi amigo, we are losing the shape of the circle.
What threads unravel in tenderness.
What time, so lived, decomposing
the very uncertainty.
What shall we do with the predictions and the foreigners?
Where has the pulchritude gone belonging to the grass?

Ah, mi amigo, from always, maybe never
we received compressed
the eruption of winter,
and each time the greener our hallucinations,
each time more visionary, the Era
that destroys and reconstructs us.
So much to do
and so little have we done!
Let's cry, and be happy,
happy for not being
for what we were
for what we might perhaps be.

Ah, mi amigo, from the voltaic arc
the most important thing:
neither you nor I are
as important as this novelty.

Ah, mi amigo, the blessed one,
let's cry again
and let's be happy.

Fuera del paraíso

Después dijimos mar
y era mentira
—RUTH LÓPEZ

I

Y era mentira. Indefensa mentira de cobardes.
Ni siquiera verdad pintarrajeada
epitafio de vieja prostituta.
También era mentira mi mentira de amianto
contra el fuego mortal.

Era mentira el miedo acuclillado
la porcelana rota
la calidad del barro.

Era mentira, piadosa ficción para el agonizante
que dijéramos *mar*
y saltaran los peces.
También dijimos arca, intención, monotipia
cualquier otro argumento.
Todos eran mentira.
Las torpes, las tristes, ineficaces, inútiles mentiras.

II

Una mujer y un hombre amanecen de espaldas
sin más antecedentes que su sexo.
Una mujer y un hombre zozobran porque faltan.
Una mujer y un hombre se juegan a los naipes la rutina
y soportan la rabia fracasada, la cópula dudosa
la ley de gravedad, la ingravidez burlona de sus leyes.
Una mujer y un hombre sin solución se asfixian.
Nos dejan como epígrafe
la tersa soledad de sus espaldas.

III

Con tanta bruma, con tanta irredención
cómo voy a decir *sol* y que me alumbre

Away from Paradise

Afterward, we said sea
and it was a lie.
—RUTH LÓPEZ

I

And it was a lie. The coward's defenseless lie.
Not even a speckled truth,
the epitaph of an old prostitute.
It was also a lie, my lie of amianthus
against the mortal fire.

It was a lie, the squatting fear,
the broken porcelain,
the quality of the clay.

It was a lie, a pious fiction for the dying one
that we said *sea*
and the fish jumped at our voices.
We also said arc, intention, monotype
or just another argument.
They were all lies.
Dumb, saddened, ineffective, futile lies.

II

A woman and a man awaken back to back
without any other precedent than their sex.
A woman and a man are sinking because they are missing.
A woman and a man play rooting out like a game of cards,
they hold the hand of their anger, the questionable copula,
the law of gravity, the mocking lightness of its laws.
A woman and a man with no solution strangle.
They leave an epitaph, the soft solitude of their backs.

III

With so much mist, with so much unrecovered,
how can I say *sun* and believe it will shine upon me,

cómo voy a decir *vivo* y despertarme
cómo decir *rasguño* y que no duela
cómo decir *mordisco*
y no irme desangrando a borbotones.

He de aclarar que soy un animal
que gritó en su momento:
hágase la luz
si la luz no se hizo
no quiero que me acusen de penumbras.

A quién ha de llegar este alarido
quién tapará mi falta de verdades
y tiemblo, tiemblo
indefensa atrapada en mis redes
volví a la tentación de las espinas
olvidé rescatar los puntos cardinales.

> I V

No ves que este agujero en desbandada
de lo que nunca fui
se consolida
y espléndido animal
me asusto en el salón de los espejos
me espanto ante la imagen crudelísima
que devuelve en su magia la linterna
y afirmo que he perdido la guerra contra el hielo.

No ves que era difícil guarecernos
si éramos exiliados
como nuestros antecesores
—los primeros declarados no gratos en el mundo—
borramos de un portazo la noción paraíso
subrayando en vigor la cláusula *vencidos*.

A quién le tocará acribillar de culpas la manzana
cuál de los dos pagará su tributo con sentencias
cuál será el perdedor
cuál el perdido.

how can I say *I am alive* and expect to awaken,
how can I say *scratch* and imagine the hurt is gone,
how can I say *bite*
and not leave here spurting blood.

I must make it clear that I am an animal
who shouted at a certain moment:
Let there be light.
If the light was not,
I don't want to be accused of darkness.

And who will my shout reach,
who will cover my lack of truth?
I tremble, tremble
without weapons, trapped in my own netting.
I returned to the temptation of the thorns.
I forgot to rescue the cardinal points.

IV

Can't you see that this routed hole
of what I never was
consolidates
and I become a splendid animal,
terrified in a room of mirrors.
And I frighten myself before the cruel image
that returns the lantern to its magic,
and I affirm that I have lost the war against the ice.

Can't you see how hard it was to protect ourselves
if we were exiles
like our ancestors — the first who were declared non grata in the
    world —
we erased, all at once, the notion of paradise
underwritten with the force of the clause that says *Defeated.*

Now whose turn is it to riddle the apple with guilt.
Which one of the two will pay tribute with judgments,
which will be the loser,
which the lost one.

Se van los que yo quiero

También te marcharás, como José.
No podré conocer tu nombre verdadero.
No podré descifrar tu santo y seña.
No podré saber nunca
en qué lugar del barrio está tu casa.

Yo no pude apostar
yo sólo puedo—a veces—dejar la nave al pairo
y me sirve de poco acunar las consignas.

Voy a moldear con barro una tinaja
para los peregrinos
para los como tú, con sus seudónimos
para los como tú, con sus angustias
de segundo orden
para pensar en ti sin que claudique el polen
mientras me asumo y quemo cortezas de naranja.

De nuevo irán de paso las hordas migratorias
gorriones de mi patio
yo tuve alguna vez posada sobre el hombro
un ave blanca.

Sólo sé que era blanca, intensamente blanca
con un ojo redondo y asombrado.

The Ones I Love Are Leaving

You will leave, too, like José.
No chance to know your real name.
Nor chance to decipher your saint's day and your sign.
Never to know which house is yours in the village.

I couldn't bet.
I could only — sometimes — free the vessel to its course.
It serves me little to rock the sayings.

I'm going to make a vase of clay
for each traveler
for the ones like you with your false names
for the ones like you with your second-class anguish
to think about you, never pollinated,
while I sit here burning the skin of oranges.

Again they will go flying, the migrating hoards
the sparrows in my backyard.
Sometimes I had over my shoulder
a white bird.

That's all I know, that it was white,
intensely white,
with one eye round and amazed.

La hora de los solos

No te pido que me dejes entrar en tu casa, amor mío,
pero entra tú en mi infinita soledad.

— RABINDRANATH TAGORE

Mi soledad de noria indivisible
sobre el puente de mando
con su visión lunar y sus prismáticos.
Mi soledad de albero incultivado
mi soledad de cactus.
Mi soledad ridícula
intemporal
anónima
como un testigo ecuánime su dedo sentencioso.
Mi soledad de arruga
de verbos
de parientes
mi soledad caudillo violada en lo más hondo.
Mi soledad arrítmica
sordomuda
epiléptica
antiquísima mi soledad mujer
mi niña soledad
mi paradoja.

The Hour of the Lonely Ones

I ask for no entry to your house, my love,
but you enter my infinite solitude.
— RABINDRANATH TAGORE

My solitude of indivisible drudgery
over the position of orders
with its moon vision and prismatics.
My solitude of uncultivated whiteness
my solitude of cactus.
My ridiculous solitude
timeless
anonymous
like a witness with accusing finger.
My solitude of wrinkles
of verbs
of relatives
my dictator's solitude raped to its depths.
My arrhythmic solitude
deaf and dumb
epileptic
ancestral solitude of my womanhood
my girlish solitude
my paradox.

Versión de lejanía

No quiero hacer enmiendas
las cosas
sobre todo esas cosas
son y son.
Un infeliz comienzo el de esta carta
pero no es mi propósito cantarle a las consignas.
Sólo voy a decirte que buscamos
un lugar en la sala para ubicar tu rostro
y reeditamos por turno tus manías.

Tanto tiempo y te escribo.
No me voy a quejar, no te preocupes.
No voy a hacer listados de miserias domésticas
carece de sentido si estamos tan clavados
a esta humedad del trópico.

Cuando miro a los hijos
les quisiera explicar que estoy en dos mitades:
si a veces contradigo, nunca estoy antagónica
que si anuncio me agoto, la piel se me marchita
estoy hasta los pelos, al borde de la histeria
quiero decir te amo, quiero hacer el amor
pero contigo.
Entonces lloro y lloro
viro al revés las fotos
que no tienen angustias, que no nos envejecen.

Después me deposito, tiemblo y vuelvo a ver claro
te invento o te imagino en los protagonistas
de los filmes del sábado.
No me veas ridícula
con la influencia cursi del cinema barato
pero creces y creces
y te veo hermosísimo en traje de campaña
me revienta el orgullo, se me inflaman los pechos

Version of Far Away

I don't want to make amends
things
most of all those things
that are and that's all.
A sad beginning the one for this letter
but it is not my purpose to sing orders.
I will tell you only that we search
for a place in the living room to put your face
and that we re-edit by turns your mania.

Such a long time and now I write to you.
No complaints don't worry.
I won't make lists of domestic miseries
it makes no sense for us nailed
to this tropical humidity.

When I look at the children
I would like to explain that I am halved:
if I sometimes contradict I'm not antagonistic
if I announce that I am exhausted, my skin fades
I'm on the brink, at the edge of hysteria
I want to say I love you, I want to make love
but with you.
Then I cry and cry
I turn the pictures backwards
the ones that show no signs of our agony, the ones that don't
    make us old.

Then I sit down, I tremble and I see again
I invent you like the star
of the Saturday films.
Don't think me ridiculous
think me vulgar, too easily influenced by cheap movies
but you grow and grow
and I see you in your handsome country attire
my pride explodes, my breasts swell

es tan fuerte ese nombre: Matagalpa:
mezcla de ron con miel para aclarar las dudas.

Quiero que estés allí.
Quiero que estemos juntos.
Lavaré las paredes (por si acaso)
me haré un vestido nuevo para cuando regreses.

Cuídate, pero no demasiado
y te amaré más virgen después de este gran parto.

it's so strong that name: Matagalpa:
a mixture of rum and honey that clears up any doubts.

I want you to be there.
I want us to be together.
I will clean the walls (just in case).
I will make myself a new dress for your return.

Take care, but not too much
and I will love you more virgin after this grand birth.

Las memorias

Ya no le quedo bien a mi ventana
no le ajusto
porque perdí mi lucidez de acequia.
No quisiera estar triste
y sin embargo
pájaro medieval que adivinó el futuro
bailé violentamente sobre el filo del hacha.

Hasta cuándo será
hasta dónde será mi propia lejanía
mis traspies, horóscopos viciados
mi angustia
cada vez más digestiva.

Si supieran
hermanos
qué perfil más borroso estoy lavando
como prenda legítima
y cuánto se me pierde en lontananza
cuánto y cuánto me observo desde lejos
y tan poco me gusto
y cuánto diera al fin por restaurarme
y restañar la cuenca de mis ojos con esmalte purísimo.

No es de malas memorias de lo que estamos hechos
es de memorias simples
pero mal compartidas.

Memories

I don't look good in my window anymore
I don't fit
because I've lost my trench lucidity.
I don't want to be sad
but still
medieval bird who guessed the future
I danced violently on the blade of the axe.

When will it be
where my own distance,
my stumbles, corrupt horoscopes,
my anguish
more digestible each time.

If only you knew
brothers
the blurred profile I'm erasing
as a legal jewel
and how it loses itself at the horizon
how I can see myself from afar
and how little I like myself
and how much I would give to restore myself
seal my eye sockets with the purest enamel.

We are not made of bad memories.
We are made of simple memories
poorly shared.

Delirio de Sor Juana por Van Gogh

Si al menos en mi cuarto cupieran girasoles.
Una silla. Sus botas. Sus camisas manchadas.
Si al menos encontrara revuelta en mis papeles
alguna de sus cartas. Pero nada.
Nada que nombre al hombre. Nada que lo acredite.
Si pudiera gritarle en tonos ocres. Alternativamente
sumarme a su navaja. Pero nada. Nada podrá impedir
que se asesine. Porque yo no estaré. Porque no he sido yo
quien dibujara trigales por sus manos.
Recurso intemporal esta agonía. Nada.
Nada que rompa el claustro. Las uñas se me quiebran
en su arritmia. Mis hábitos son grises. Deplorables.
La celda se estremece. Pero nada.
Nadie podrá impedir que se asesine.
No llegan cataclismos a mi altura. Las barreras no saltan.
Si al menos en mi cuarto cupieran girasoles
no estaría desangrándose. Taciturno. Frenético.
Sobre el inerte campo de la reina de espadas.

Delirium of Sor Juana for Van Gogh

If only sunflowers would fit in my bedroom.
A chair. His boots. His stained shirts.
If at least I could find, lost among my papers,
one of his letters. But nothing.
Nothing to name the man. Nothing to make him real.
If I could yell to him in ochre tones. Alternately
add myself to his razor. But nothing. Nothing can impede
his suicide. Because I would not be there. Because I wasn't
the one who drew wheat fields through his hands.
Timeless resource, this agony. Nothing.
Nothing to break this cloister. My nails are breaking
in their arrhythmia. My habits are gray. Deplorable.
The cell shudders. But nothing.
Nobody can impede his suicide.
There are no cataclysms arriving at my height. The barriers
cannot jump. If only sunflowers would fit in my bedroom
he wouldn't be bleeding. Taciturn. Frenetic.
Over the inert country of the Queen of Spades.

Hija de Eva

Queredlas cual las hacéis

—SOR JUANA INÉS DE LA CRUZ

Ay, hombre, por qué espantas
la cándida estructura de la hierba
por qué desacreditas la piel de las naranjas
si entre mi desnudez y el artificio
prefiero arar desnuda las viñas de la ira
que andar ejercitando los roles que me imponen.

Yo soy un ejemplar que no me canto
y menos me celebro
lo que diga de mí es solamente mío.
Unicamente en ti vuelve mi cuerpo a ser
el molde para el pan de nuestros días.
¿Qué esperabas de mí?
¿Que apareciera cubierta de acertijos?
¿Que jugara al insecto inapresable
cuando mi sexo ardía acechando el contacto
de tus manos?
¿Esperabas quizás que pestañeara púdica,
y que luego, a escondidas, pensando en ti,
varón, me masturbase?
¿Te sorprende escuchar una palabra dura?
Una canción de cuna también puedo cantarte
y puedo redimirme ante tus piernas
y llorar
llorar por la verdad
haciéndonos saltar desprevenidos.

Espejismo verbal es mi amuleto
contra este mar feroz y apocalíptico
donde temprano o tarde naufragamos.
Contra la roca el cuerpo
y el corazón también contra la roca.

Daughter of Eve

Wanting them the way you make them.
— SOR JUANA INÉS DE LA CRUZ

Ay, hombre, why do you frighten
the candid structure of the grass
why do you discredit the skin of the orange
between my nudity and the masquerade
I'd rather plow the vineyards of rage naked
than wander living the lives you'd give me.

I am a character who doesn't brag
much less do I applaud myself
what I say of myself is mine alone.
Only in you do I become the mold
for our daily bread.
What did you expect?
That I appear covered in riddles?
That I play the illusive insect
while my sex, afire, awaits the touch of your hands?
Were you hoping, perhaps, for me to blink innocently,
and then, while hiding, think about you,
male, and masturbate?
Does it surprise you to hear a harsh word?
I can also sing to you a lullaby
I can redeem myself at your feet
and cry
cry for the truth
that makes us both spring up alarmed.

My token's a mirage made of words
against this ocean, fierce and apocalyptic
where sooner or later we will shipwreck.
Against the rock the body
and the heart also against the rock.

Intimidad y Fuga

Puedo escribir los versos amargos de esta noche.
Escribir desamor, paráfrasis, nostalgia,
color local, cualquiera es mariposa,
cualquiera puede amar a su rival hasta el cansancio.
   Cuidado.
Puede ser un conflicto
que una mujer desnude sus íntimos alardes,
que una mujer no mienta,
que desista de maquillar el gesto para salir a escena,
que diga estoy frustrada en el centro del ring,
que haga regulaciones en el mapa,
que se confiese adúltera,
que cuente sus problemas personales.

Ser una mujer   sin adjetivos
puede ser un trastorno porque
se compromete el misterio de su sexo
si confiesa tener treinta y dos años
y sus días de histeria y anorgasmia.

Si quiere deambular,   encontrar la equidad,
la proporción exacta,
evitar el estigma
o cualquier otro riesgo
es muy   pero muy probable
que sea   una mujer pública.

Intimacy and Fugue

I can write the bitter verses of this night.
To write unloving, paraphrase, longing,
local color, anyone is a butterfly,
anyone can love the rival to exhaustion.
   Be careful.
It can be a conflict
when a woman strips herself of her most intimate pretensions,
when a woman does not lie,
when she desists in making up gestures on stage,
when she says I quit in the middle of the ring,
when she redraws the map,
when she confesses to adultery,
when she tells her personal problems.

To be a woman   without adjectives
can be disturbing because
the mystery of her sex is compromised
if she confesses to being thirty-two,
speaks aloud of her days of hysteria and *anorgasmia*.

If she wants to roam about,   find equity,
the exact proportion,
to avoid stigma
or any other risk
it's very   but very probable
that she's   a woman for the public.

Afuera está lloviendo

Mis pobres pies, tan cansados . . .
                                        — JOSÉ MARTÍ

Afuera está lloviendo
y desempolvo
una suma total de soledades.
Magnifico los cambios pero sigo
atónita, distante, perdida entre dos mundos
bordando paralelos que mal me justifiquen.

Magnifico los cambios
y no es más que el vacío mortal en mis caderas
no es más que este inventario de escombros
donde incluyo
mi sed de mujer sola
con todo el desamparo de mi sexo.

Afuera está lloviendo
y mis pies, tan cansados:
sabuesos disputándose rastrojos de ternura.

Afuera está lloviendo
y adentro
estoy tan sola.

It's Raining Outside

My poor feet, so tired . . .
— JOSÉ MARTÍ

It's raining outside
and I am dusting
the total sum of solitudes.
I magnify the changes but I continue
perplexed, distant, lost between two worlds
embroidering parallels that might justify me wrong.

I magnify the changes
and it is nothing but the mortal emptiness of my hips
not more than this inventory of rubble
where I include
the thirst of a woman alone
with all the abandonment of my sex.

It's raining outside
and my feet, so tired:
bloodhounds disputing stubbles of tenderness.

It's raining outside
and inside
I am alone.

Poema sin guitarra

Necesito
tener una guitarra y sorprenderte
si es que la soledad exhibe su victoria
sobre el campo arrasado que es tu cuerpo.

Necesito esa música
con sus correspondientes avanzadas
sus tácticas, también sus estrategias
y los preparativos para el acto final
que es la derrota.

Necesito tan sólo tener una guitarra
y muchos años menos
menos pedazos
arriesgados en vano en otra escaramuza
para quebrar tu cerco
salmodiando un versículo
o un sálvate de toda tentación al olvido.

Necesito escribir
tener una guitarra y sorprenderte.

Poem without a Guitar

I need
to have a guitar and to surprise you
that is if solitude's victorious
throughout the devastated country of your body.

I need the music
with its forward corresponding moves
its tactics and its strategies
and preparations for the final act
which is defeat.

I need only a guitar
and fewer years
fewer pieces
risked in vain in another skirmish
to break down your wall
chanting a verse
or a Salvat from every temptation of forgetting.

I need to write
have a guitar and surprise you.

Acertijo

En este cuarto
testigo a voz en cuello de mis conspiraciones
arriesgo las barajas de la suerte
o de la mala suerte.
En este cuarto
testigo mudo del más legal de todos
mis amores culpables
redacto un ultimátum
preparo un regicidio.

En este cuarto
decreto una inmersión
sin admitir ningún sobreviviente.
En este cuarto fraguo la rebelión del cuerpo
firmo un acta de paz y me derramo
los nervios calcinados
y el córazon en crisis
al próximo combate.

Riddle

Inside this room
speechless witness of my conspiracies
I risk the cards of luck
or bad luck.
Inside this room
mute witness of the most legal of all
my guilty loves
I dictate an ultimatum
I prepare a final record.

Inside this room
I decree an immersion
without securing a survival.
Inside this room I forge a rebellion of the body
I sign notes for peace and I spread
my hardened nerves
and my heart in crisis
to the next combat.

Caleidoscopio

Allí estábamos todos:
el que cayó marcado por la tromba
el que arruinó su estampa por inepto
el que no abrió una brecha
y violó la ciudad en estado de sitio.
El que sufrió el pecado de la clarividencia
el que abonó con heces estrambóticas
el que no pudo dar más clavos al martirio
el que no llegó a tiempo a las demoliciones
el que llegó temprano
el que no vino
y le basta decir que no se le informó.

Allí estábamos todos:
los inocentes por desconocimiento
y los culpables por legal ignorancia
los cómplices más cultos
los que se alimentaban de prejuicios
los más elaborados
los más cíclicos
los cantores del tono rezagado
los ciegos a fuerza de no querer mirar
los sujetos acríticos
los críticos sujetos a sus dogmas
los denominadores con sus tábulas rasas
los fachadas invictas
los espaldas marcadas.

Allí estábamos todos
esperando medallas y sentencias.

Kaleidoscope

All of us were there:
the one who fell marked by the water jet
the one who ruined his countenance through ineptitude
the one who did not strike a flame
and violated the city in martial law.
The one who suffered the sin of clairvoyance
the one who fertilized with bizarre feces
the one who could not give more nails to the torture
the one who was not on time for the demolitions
the one who came early
the one who didn't come
and resolved by saying he wasn't informed.

All of us were there:
the innocent ones because they didn't know
and the guilty ones for legal ignorance
the more cultivated accomplices
the ones who fed themselves with prejudices
the more elaborated ones
the more cyclic ones
the singers with the lagger tone
the blind blind from not wanting to see
the ones subject to criticism
the critics subject to their dogmas
the denominators with their tabula rasa
the unbeaten facade
the marked backs

All of us were there
waiting for medals and judgments.

Balada por la sangre sin pretexto

Melisma era la sangre. Diagrama cardinal en el prontuario.
Rito de sangre. Ausencia. Es decir: sin presente.
Era la sangre. Hermano. La sangre de dolernos.
Crucifixión del coágulo. La sangre yerta. Tísica. Hecha vapor.
Hartándose sedienta sobre el barro. Lamiendo el horizonte
sin cansarse. Una vez. Otra vez. ¿Hasta cuándo?
¿Hasta cuándo será rojísimo el festín? Salpicadura cruel
la de este charco. Sangre. Sangre. Sangre que sume el párpado.
Enceguece. Maceración perpetua de cartílagos.
Inútilmente evoco el trino de mis pájaros.
¿Qué se han hecho mis pájaros? Entonces. Sin remedio.
He perdido mis verdes. Mis azules. Ya nunca serán más
que distantes. Distintivos. Lavados por la sangre
de un rojo sin amparo. Era la sangre. Hermano.
La sangre en espiral batiendo su abanico.
Su don de ubicuidad. Su salto. La piel con su vertiente
en dos orillas perfectamente claras. La tierra calcinante.
Bebiéndome a zarpazos. ¿Dónde dejó mi aliento?
¿Dónde empiezo a doblarme de rodillas?
¿De dónde llega el eco del último disparo?

Ballad for the Blood without Pretext

Melisma was the blood. Cardinal diagram in the compendium.
Ritual of blood. Absence. I mean: without presence.
It was the blood. Brother. The blood of hurting ourselves.
Crucifixion of the clot. The stiffened blood. Tubercular.
Made vapor. Feeding up thirsty over the clay. Licking the horizon
without tiring. Once. Again. Until when?
When will the feast be red? Cruel splash,
the one from this puddle. Blood. Blood. Blood that submerges
the eyelid. It blinds. Perpetual maceration of cartilage.
Hopeless, I evoke the warblings of my birds.
What's happened to my birds? Then. Without remedies.
And I have lost my greens. My blues. They will never be anything
but distant. Distinctive. Washed by the blood
of a red without refuge. It was the blood. Brother.
The spiral blood beating its fan.
Its skill for being everywhere. Its jump. The skin with its
    wounds,
two perfect clear edges. The burned earth.
Drinking me in one gulp. Where was my breath?
Where did it begin bending me to my knees?
From which direction comes the echo of the last shot?

Brindis

Añejo. Añejo el corazón. Mi vino rancio
de esporas maltratadas. Humus de siempreviva
que se acoda en la esquina de un pañuelo.
Destila lento. Lento. Sumerjo el corazón.
Lo añejo en los toneles. Un. Dos. Un. Dos.
Lento. Lento. Cansancio.
Artesa rebosante de estirpe sin sosiego.
Penúltimo reducto. Sorpresas y temblores.
Añejo ya. Y agrio. Y dolorido. Arrítmico. Violento.
El vaso donde bebo mi corazón que es vino.
El vaso en el que ofrezco mi corazón que es vino.
El vino en que me brindo y me derramo.
Añejo el vino. El corazón añejo. Sin rótulo.
Sin margen. Sin amparo. Mi añejo corazón.
Sin garantías. Carral dudoso que arrastra la marea.
Enemigo leal que a lentos sorbos bebo.
Que a lentos sorbos brindo.
Botín que se disputan los corsarios.
Mi añejo corazón escancian en sus copas.
Entre riscos y hogueras. Como un himno de espanto.

A Toast

Aged. Aged the heart. My rancid wine
of spores mishandled. Humus of everlasting flowers
bordering the corner of a handkerchief.
It distills slowly. Slowly. I submerge my heart.
I age it inside the barrels. One. Two. One. Two.
Slowly. Slowly. Exhaustion.
Overflowing trough, the tireless bloodline.
Penultimate redoubt. Temblors and surprises.
Aged already. And sour. And in pain. Arrhythmic. Violent.
The glass where I drink, my heart, is wine.
The glass in which I offer my heart is wine,
and the wine with which I toast myself and scatter me.
Aged the wine. The heart, aged. Without a tag.
Without a margin. Without shelter. My aged heart.
Without guarantees. Suspicious wine barrel dragged by the tide.
Faithful enemy I drink slowly.
To which I toast in slow sips.
Booty that the corsairs dispute.
My aged heart fills your glasses.
Between cliffs and fires. Like a frightening hymn.

El ángel caído

Mira. David.
Cómo se encrespan los últimos corceles de la tarde.
Cómo se insubordinan.
Cómo aclaman triunfantes las voraces trompetas.
Pero ya no recuerdo cómo llegan las cosas a nombrarse.
Pero es que ya no sé.
Se me pudren de infamia las prendas de ir viviendo.
Y soy un ángel más.
Un ángel que se agota. En la corte agotada de los ángeles.
Mira. David.
Como se agitan los corceles finales. Como acuden al grito
triunfal de la trompeta.
Anuncian que hay que huir. No importa a dónde.
No importa a que país de miniaturas. No importa a qué proyecto.
O espejismo. Yo sólo quiero huir.
Evadir los escombros del íntimo desastre.
Si pudiera negarles el don de la palabra. Es que han mentido
tanto.
Y soy un ángel roto dejándose rodar por las alcantarillas.
El agua inmunda es sólo una verdad viciada entre tanta mentira.
Migajas. Sólo nombro migajas. Es muy serio cumplir treinta y
siete años
Y ser un ángel roto. Violento de llorar en la vigilia.

The Fallen Angel

Look. David.
How the last steeds of the afternoon curl.
How they subjugate themselves.
How the trumpets acclaim triumphantly.
But I cannot remember how things are named.
I don't know anymore.
My clothes are rotten from infamy.
And I am but another angel.
An angel that is exhausting himself. In the tired court of angels.
Look. David.
How the final steeds agitate.
How they come to the triumphal scream of the trumpet.
They announce that we must escape.
No matter where.
No matter to what country of miniatures. No matter for what
    mission.
Or mirage. I want only to escape.
To evade the ruins of intimate disaster.
If I could deny them the gift of the word.
They have lied so much. And I am
a broken angel letting myself stumble through sewers.
The filthy water contaminates truth among so many lies.
Crumbs. I can name only crumbs. It is a serious thing to be
thirty-seven and be a broken angel. Violent from crying in the
    vigil.

Huérfanos y cómplices

Debimos ser más bellos, más exactos,
en la ascención perenne
desesperada y tierna. Complejísima.
Cantores de lo abstracto
qué podíamos hacer con el paralelismo
de lo que   siendo nuestro
      no nos pertenecía
si dejamos al azar jugar con los designios.

No había vocación de jardineros
no tuvimos   la diestra interferencia de la luna.
Nos dimos a la trampa por la trampa
en cómplice orfandad con los desheredados
con los que no profesan
con los que no convergen
y arropan en su cuerpo todas las religiones.
Confundimos la luz con la bombilla
quedándonos a ras   en plena superficie.

Cazadores sin dotes, abortivos,
las liebres aprendieron
      y ahora nos persiguen.

Orphans and Accomplices

We should have been more beautiful, more exact
in the perennial ascension,
desperate and tender. Complicated.
Singers of the abstract,
what could we do with the double truth
of so much   that was ours
     though nothing belonged to us
if we let chance play with the design.

We had no vocation for gardening
nor did we have   the skillful interference of the moon.
We gave into the trap for the trap
in complicity with the disinherited
the ones that do not profess
the ones that do not converge
who wrap their bodies in all religions.
We mistook the bulb for the light
floating eye level   on the plain surface.

Hunters without dowry, abortives,
the hares learned
     and now they follow us.

Legado

a Mariela, mi hija

Si alguna herencia puedo
es el amor   y el odio necesario,
un país de fermentos y raíces
una guía que explique como se producen las catástrofes
su génesis,
por qué la mala división de la alegría
y lo más importante:
para qué la esperanza
la esperanza que da   amar todo lo amable
y odiar   lo estrictamente odiable.

No puedo regalarte camafeos
ni muñecas con lazos
ni una abuela blanquísima en una mecedora;

sólo puedo legarte la ira,
la búsqueda incesante de los detonadores
un precario equilibrio para andar cuesta arriba,
la vocación del faro
y una pasión de vidrio intransferible.

Legacy

to Mariela, my daughter

If there is an inheritance I can offer you
it is love   and the necessary hate,
a country of fermentation and roots,
a guide explaining just how catastrophes happen,
their genesis,
why the bad divisions of happiness,
and most important
why Hope,
the hope that brings   to love all that is loveable
and to hate   the strictly hateful.

I can't give you cameos
or dolls with bows
or a pure white grandmother in a rocking chair.

I can only leave you rage,
the incessant search for detonators,
a dangerous equilibrium to walk up the hill,
the vocation of the lighthouse
and an untransferable glass passion.

Nocturno

Va a oscurecer. El disco anunciador de la penumbra desciende
apenas. Quedo. Dándole paso
a otra rara estación para el olvido. Olvidar. Olvidar es
la vocación perfecta. El acabado oficio.
El tierno orfebre pule. Vuelve a pulir
las acabadas prendas con que adorna el olvido.
Va a oscurecer. La calma se desliza. Sin luz. Sin timoneles.
Se va mi mocedad. Las mejores palabras
serán las que no escriba. Las que no escuche nadie. Oscurecer.
Oscuro. Temblor de niño solo que teme a que oscurezca.
La nave es ancha. Ancha.
La sombra de los árboles describen jugarretas.
El orfebre. El artífice
labora con paciencia su hermosa filigrana.
Va a anochecer. La bruma que desciende es el olvido.
La vocación perfecta.

Nocturnal

It's going to get dark. The disc announcing dusk
hardly descends. I stay. Giving space
to another rare season of forgetting. To forget. Forgetting is
the perfect vocation. The finished work.
The tender goldsmith polishes. Keeps on polishing
the finished jewels with which he adorns his forgetting.
It's going to get dark. Calm slides. Unlit. Unhelmed.
My young years are leaving. The best words
will be those I do not write. The ones no one will hear.
  Darkening.
Dark. The trembling of a lonesome child afraid it will be dark.
The vessel is wide. Wider.
The shadows of the trees describe games.
The goldsmith. The artist
labors with patience his beautiful filigree.
It's going to get dark. Forgetting is the descending mist.
The perfect vocation.

Declaraciones

I

Este papel se dobla
no soporta la intensa gravedad de la sorpresa
ni la alucinación por sobrecargas.

La estación es perfecta—
como imperfecto es el descaro del agua.

Dónde voy a secar mis prendas personales
dónde voy a encontrar un plomo para el péndulo
cómo voy a saber, ¿quién me lo explica?
qué tránsito ascendente me revuelca
qué mitad de limpieza estoy jugando
cuando beso a mis hijos y disgrego.

Amor mío, que estás
o que no estás
no puedo detenerme
no puedo ser correcta y sólo amante.
No podemos pintar corazones con tiza en las aceras.

II

No es que nos pase nada específicamente.
Sucede que es domingo en *D* mayúscula
y ya no queden cuerdas que atolondren.
No han muerto los que amo
no se ha marchado nadie en estos días
pero se acaba el año
y me sobran intangibles.
No sé quemar incienso
no puedo exorcizar esta tristeza
que se adhiere triunfante a los dobleces
y declaro mi asombro en tanto vida y vida
me arrugan el costado y lo más puro.

Declarations

I

This paper folds.
It doesn't tolerate the rapt gravity of surprises,
nor overload of hallucinations.

The season is perfect—
as wrong as the indolence of water.

Where am I going to dry my intimate garments
where am I going to find lead for the pendulum
how am I going to know, who can explain?
What ascending transit stirs me
what half-clean thing do I play with
when I kiss my children and disappear.

My love, who is
and who is not
I can't stop myself
I can't be correct and merely lover.
We can't paint hearts with chalk on the sidewalks.

II

It's not that something specific is happening to us.
It happens that it is Sunday with a capital *S*.
There isn't any music to bewilder us.
The other ones I love aren't dead.
These days no one has gone away
but the year is ending
and I have an excess of intangibles.
I don't know how to burn incense.
I can't exorcise my sadness
that clings so triumphantly to the folds
I declare my surprise while life and life
wrinkles my side and the purest part.

III

Sucede que las horas se agrupan monocordes
con su arrullo de víctimas.
Suceden las promesas
y la desesperanza del complicado antílope.
Sucede que andan sueltos
la antorcha, el querubín
y los apóstatas.
Sucede que no eres
que no has estado nunca
que nunca llegarás
y me crece el rosario de esperar
y esperarte
mientras cultivo aristas en el jardín ajeno.

III

It happens that the hours gather in monochords
the victims' lullaby.
Promises happen
like a desperate antelope.
And it happens they walk by themselves,
the torch, the cherubim
and the apostates.
It happens that you are not,
that you have never been
that you will never come
and the rosary grows on me
waiting for you
while I grow weeds in someone else's garden.

Despedida del ángel

Enfermo de traición. De realidad. Contemplo desde lejos
la intensa llamarada de las naves. Todo lo limpia el fuego.
Todo lo purifica. Un alarido grave clavado en la garganta.
Las llamas lamen lentas los flancos de las naves.
¿Y dónde está el traidor? ¿Y quién es el culpable?
Atisbo la penumbra y tanta oscuridad me desorienta.
La calma es un manojo de apariencia.
Me castiga el dolor de los maderos. Los maderos crujientes
lamentándose. Qué falta me hace un himno. Un nuevo Dios.
Otra bandera. Otra razón de ser y nuevos ángeles.
Ya nadie necesita mis papeles. Ternura para dos mis torpes
    garabatos.
Crepitan en la hoguera mis sueños infantiles. Simulacro de
    juego.
El peligroso juego de armar la despedida.
Pero es mucho peor. Pero me engaño.
A la ascensión llegué sin estar listo. Entre una trampa y otra
me robaron la fuerza. La amable lucidez de mis brebajes.
Me robaron las notas del *Canto a la Alegría.*
Si soy hombre. O mujer. Ya no me importa.
Tampoco ser un ángel podrido de cansancio.
Me acuchillan la fe. Me acuchillan la carne.
Se reparten las sobras del festín de palabras. Sólo tuve palabras.
Para nombrar dolores. Para nombrar los males. Y palabras de
    amor
que magnifican. Qué caro cuesta todo. Qué caro cobran todos
los ritos celestiales. Enfermo de traición el ángel se despide.
La realidad comienza a destruirse en la pira siniestra de sus
    naves.

The Angel's Farewell

Sick of betrayal. Of reality. I watch from afar
the true flames of the vessels. Fire cleans everything.
It purifies. A grave howl nailed in the throat.
The flames lick the flanks of the vessels.
And where is the traitor? Who is the guilty one?
I see the dusk. The obscure confuses me.
This calm is just a handful of masks.
The pain of the wood punishes me. The wood splits
lamenting. How badly I need a hymn now. A new God.
A new flag. Another reason for being and new angels.
No one needs my papers. Have tenderness for two for my clumsy
    scrawls.
My childhood dreams are heaped on the bonfire. Fake game.
The dangerous game of arming a farewell.
It is worse than that. But I deceive myself.
I ascended but wasn't ready. Between one trap and another
my power was stolen. And my potions' amiable lucidity.
The notes of *The Song of Happiness* were stolen, also.
Were I a man. Were I a woman. I don't care anymore.
Were I an angel putrefied from exhaustion.
They stab my faith. They stab my skin.
They scatter the leftover feast of words. I had only words.
To name sorrows. To name the wicked. And words of love
that magnify. Everything is too expensive. Too expensive
all the celestial rites. Sick of betrayal the angel says its farewell.
What is real begins burning on the sad pyre of its vessels.

Invocación

Estoy como la casa del guardabosque
donde el hacha es la culpa y los árboles caen.
— LINA DE FERIA

Nadie llama a mi puerta. Nadie viene a golpearme.
A maldecirme. A quererme. A llorar en mi mano.
Nadie se ruboriza si blasfemo. Si reniego de Dios.
Y ya sin nombre me vuelvo hacia la puerta
de par en par bloqueada en su mutismo.
Nadie comparte mi destino de andén. De guardavía.
De guijarro olvidado. De brizna confundida.
Nadie se compromete con mi estado de sitio.
Afuera hay una luz. Una ventana abierta.
Mi puerta. Su mudez. Su fiereza de hierro.
Es mi designio.
Asusta este silencio del que nadie me salva.
La próxima estación
también era mentira.

Invocation

I am the ranger station
where the hatchet is guilty and the trees are falling.
— LINA DE FERIA

Nobody knocks at my door. Nobody comes to hit me.
To curse me. To want me. To cry in my hands.
Nobody blanches if I blaspheme.
If I deny God. Already without a name
I return to the door boarded up, mute.
Nobody shares my platform destiny. Of railway guard.
Of a forgotten pebble. Of a confused string.
Nobody's obliged to my house arrest.
Outside, a light. An open window.
My door. Its muteness. Its iron fierceness.
This is my destiny.
This silence from which no one saves me frightens me.
The next station was also a lie.

Poema del hondero

Estoy lanzando piedras contra la oreja sorda.
Cambiante de ambos mundos.
Esto es la soledad y sus crepitaciones.
Estoy haciendo señas junto al tonto paciente que yace en la
    colina.
Y con la pobre loca que remienda sus cuitas en el banco del
    parque.
Por sus dedos conclusos. De tejedora rota. Destilan los retazos.
La crónica final del abandono. Le digo que me espere.
No es tiempo de morir a la sombra marchita de los álamos.
Estoy lanzando piedras contra la oreja sorda.
Sangrante de este mundo.
Este mundo convexo que muestra sus espaldas.
Se extraviaron los planos que ayuden a escapar del laberinto.
Estoy lanzando piedras: soy la loca del parque.
Soy el tonto decrépito que yace en la colina.
Soy la canción fatal a Eleanor Rigby.
Y soy la antología de los que mueren solos. Sin traspasar el
    túnel.
Sigo lanzando piedras. Estoy cansada y sigo.
La loca muestra impúdica la mueca desdentada de su hastío.
Vira al revés su bolso. Esparce pieza a pieza su manojo de
    olvidos.
Le digo que me espere.
No es tiempo de morir a la sombra marchita de los álamos.
No resisto esta paz de abrevadero. Ni la culpa redonda
pendiente del manzano. Ni la flecha buscando centro en mi
    cabeza.
Estoy lanzando piedras. Quizás encuentren eco.
O las devore el fondo.

Poem for a Slinger

I am throwing stones against a deaf ear.
Interchangeable in two worlds.
This is what solitude is and its crepitations.
I am signing to the dumb patient who lies on the hill.
And to the poor crazy woman who mends her grief on the park
  bench.
To her closed fingers. The poor broken weaver.
Her remnants of cloth are distilling. The last chronicle
of abandonment. I tell her to wait for me.
This is not the time to die, in the withered shadows of poplars.
I am throwing stones against a deaf ear.
Bleeding from the world.
This backwards world that turns its back.
Lost the map that shows a way out from the labyrinth.
I am throwing stones. I am the crazy woman at the park.
I am the stupid old man who lies on the hill.
I am the fatal song to Eleanor Rigby.
And I am the anthology of the ones dying alone. Without
passing through the tunnel. I keep on throwing stones. I am
  tired
but I go on. The crazy woman shows with immodesty
the toothless grimace of her tedium. She turns her bag upside
  down.
Scatters piece by piece her handfuls of forgettings.
I ask her to wait for me.
This is no time to die, in the withered shadows of poplars.
I don't resist this irrigating peace. Nor the round guilt
hanging from the apple tree. Nor the arrow
aimed at the center of my head.
I am throwing stones. Maybe they'll find an echo.
Maybe they'll be devoured by the depth.

El ángel agotado

Parece. Sí. Apenas una sombra descolgándose. Y quién lo iba a
    decir.

Quién lo dijera. Torvo pájaro lame las llagas del rapsoda.

La mitad que no soy se contamina. Parece. Sí. Y quién lo iba a
    decir.

Quién lo creyera. Ante quién puedo hacer valer mis actas
de inocencia. Apenas una sombra y se levantan.

Apenas una sombra y se encabritan. Parece. Sí.

Muy tarde. Muy tarde para todo.

Los mejores fantasmas de mí se insubordinan. "El pájaro que
    come.

El que mira comer." Pájaro que vigila las cuencas despojadas
de su víctima. El pájaro testigo anunciatorio. El pájaro.

Su rol protagonista. Y quién lo iba a decir. Quién fue el heraldo.

Qué oráculo predijo la sucesión de espectros. Apenas una
    sombra.

Una suave amenaza. Y se presentan turbios mis arcanos mayores.

Enrojecen. Se encrespan pertinaces visiones obsesivas. Y ya
no puedo más con los sueños de sangre. Parece ser muy tarde.

Muy tarde para todo. Y quién lo iba a decir.

La duda sólo sirve de pasto a la certeza. Parece. Sí. Muy tarde.

El pájaro mejor se desespera atrapado en cieno pegajoso del
    fondo.

Apenas una sombra. Escaleras de naipes prestos a derrumbarse.

El pez entra en las redes con un temblor atónito.

Las redes son un antro. Y te aprisionan. Torvo pájaro espía
al pájaro apacible. Al obstinado pájaro de las ensoñaciones.

Parece. Sí. Que nadie me perdona.

El pájaro acentúa sus rasgos de cansancio.

El ángel otra vez se desanima. Y quién lo iba a decir.

Quién lo creyera. Apenas una sombra que empieza a
    descolgarse.

Y ya se espantan. Raudas. Las legiones de pájaros.

The Exhausted Angel

It seems. Yes. Barely a shadow descending. And who would have
   said it.
Who could tell. Fierce bird licks the wound of the rhapsodist.
The half part I am not contaminates. It seems. Yes.
And who would have said it. Who would believe it. Before whom
can I assert my innocent acts. Barely a shadow and they are
   standing.
Barely a shadow and they are furious. It seems. Yes.
Very late. Too late for everything.
The best ghosts within me start rebelling. "The bird that eats.
The one that watches." The bird observing the bowls left
by his victim. The witness bird that announces. The bird.
His protagonist role. And who would have said it. Who was the
   herald.
What oracle predicted this succession of ghosts. Barely a
   shadow.
A soft threat. And now my oldest arcane things present
   themselves in confusion.
They blush. Obsessive visions curl persistently.
And I cannot resist anymore my blood dreams. It seems
too late. Too late for everything. And who would have said it.
Doubts only serve as grass to certainty. It seems. Yes. Too late.
The best bird trapped in the depths' sticky ooze
becomes desperate. Barely a shadow. Stairs of cards ready to fall.
The fish enters the nets with amazed trembling.
The nets are a cavern. They jail you. A fierce bird spies
on the serene bird. On the obstinate bird of enchantments.
It seems. Yes. That no one forgives me.
The bird exaggerates his gestures of fatigue. Again,
the angel is exhausted. And who would have said it.
Who would believe. Barely a shadow begins to descend.
And already flying frightened away. In torrents. The legions of
   birds.

Última hora

Nadie podrá esconderse en los badajos
cuando suenen las treinta campanadas.
Nadie traerá un reflejo dorado en la pupila.
Nadie confesará que el eslabón perdido
estuvo entre sus manos
y que pudo una vez—aunque sea una vez—
enderezar el rumbo.
Nadie dirá que pudo ser mejor—
pero el tic-tac, las cuentas, los ajustes . . .
Nadie, nadie vendrá con amuletos
y veremos sus rostros
pintados con asombro en los carteles.
Nadie dirá: *Yo soy la penúltima palabra.*
No habrá clemencia con los que se equivoquen.
Ni el suicida turístico de la ruleta rusa podrá salir ileso.
Ni el vendedor de alarmas
podrá expedir nuevos certificados
funcionales y apócrifos.
Ni el homicida esteta
podrá sumarse al curso de los perseguidores.
Ni el ciudadano—agenda podrá
marcar las pautas del domingo.
El escriba
no enmendará su falta de coraje ortográfico
y los inversionistas ilusorios
no cubrirán su culpa con el horario ajeno.

The Last Hour

Nobody can hide among the clappers
sounding thirty bell strokes.
Nobody will carry a golden reflection in the eye.
Nobody will confess that the lost link
was ever in his hands
and for once, just once,
he could straighten the course.
Nobody will say that it could have been better—
but the tick-tock and the counts and the adjustments . . .
No, nobody will come with amulets to see
their own astounded faces
painted on the posters.
Nobody will say: *I'm the penultimate word.*
There will be no clemency for the mistaken.
Even the suicidal tourist of the Russian roulette
will not come through uninjured.
Nor can the alarm seller expedite new functional,
apocryphal certificates.
Nor can the aesthete murderer
be added to the persecutors' course.
Nor can the citizen's agenda
mark the rules on Sundays.
The scribe
will not amend his failure of orthographic courage,
nor will the schedules of others cover the guilt
of the illusory investors.

Testamento

Ha llegado mi madre, rociándome el umbral
de agua bendita. La miro acontecer.

Sonrío quedo. De nada sirve. Digo. Pero callo.

Las manos de mi madre. Hace más de tres décadas
anidaron ternura en mis pañales.
Ahora sueltan mi pelo. Presurosas. Ahora quieren salvarme.

De nada sirve. Digo. Pero callo.

Por aquí pasan todos sin quedarse.
Por aquí van pasando:
mi madre es un testigo tenaz en mi agonía.

Mi madre. La que nunca leyó a Miguel Hernández.
La que bebió a Vallejo entre mis versos.
Sin saber qué bebía. Y quiere hablar con Dios.

Presentarle un recurso de Habeas Corpus
mientras trajina, dislocados los ojos,
rociándome el pudor de agua bendita.

De nada sirve. Digo. Pero callo.

Pobre madre mi madre.
Despedaza su furia contra todo. Magnífica embestida.
Sabe que no hay remedios para curar mis males.
Pero reza. Las gotas que reparte por mi cuarto
más bien parecen lágrimas de ira. Ella quiere batirse
con todos los demonios. Despojarme del mal.

Y yo la dejo hacer. De nada sirve. Digo. Pero callo.

Y le está hablando a Dios como al vecino:
lo quiere convencer con un torpe alegato

Testament

My mother has arrived sprinkling my threshold
with holy water. I see her act.

I smile still. It's no use. I say. In silence.

My mother, her hands. For more than three decades
they nested tenderness among my clothes.
Now they loosen my hair. Hurried. Now they want to save me.

It's no use. I say. In silence.

Through here everyone passes by without staying.
Through here they are passing by;
my mother, tenacious witness to my agony.

My mother. The one who never read Miguel Hernández.
The one who drank Vallejo in my verses.
Without knowing she was drinking. And she wants to speak to
    God.
To present him with a writ of Habeas Corpus
while she walks back and forth, her eyes everywhere
sprinkling my chastity with holy water.

It's no use. I say. In silence.

Poor mother my mother.
She breaks her fury against everything. Magnificent attack.
She knows there are no remedies to cure my wrongs.
But she prays. The drops she scatters in my bedroom
seem more like tears of rage. She wants to battle
all the demons. Strip me of evil.

And I let her. It's no use. I say. In silence.

And she is talking to God as if to a neighbor:
she wants to convince him with a dim allegation

A Note About the Translators

Mairym Cruz-Bernal was born in 1963 in Mayagüez, Puerto Rico. She graduated from Loyola University in New Orleans and holds an MFA in Creative Writing from Vermont College. A translator and columnist, Cruz-Bernal is the author of a book of poems in Spanish, *Poemas para no morir*, and is currently completing a book of poems in English, *On Her Face the Light of the Moon*. She lives in San Juan, and is the mother of two children.

Deborah Digges is the author of several books of poetry—most recently, *Rough Music*—and a memoir, *Fugitive Spring*. She teaches at Tufts University and lives in Amherst, Massachusetts.